No Minor Chords

Also by André Previn

Music Face to Face
Orchestra
André Previn's Guide to the Orchestra

ANDRÉ PREVIN

No
Minor
Chords

MY DAYS IN HOLLYWOOD

DOUBLEDAY

New York   London   Toronto   Sydney   Auckland

PUBLISHED BY DOUBLEDAY
a division of
Bantam Doubleday Dell Publishing Group, Inc.
666 Fifth Avenue, New York, New York 10103

DOUBLEDAY and the portrayal of an anchor
with a dolphin are trademarks of Doubleday,
a division of Bantam Doubleday Dell Publishing Group, Inc.

Library of Congress Cataloging-in-Publication Data

Previn, André, 1929–
No minor chords : my days in Hollywood / André Previn. — 1st ed.
    p.   cm.
1. Previn, André, 1929- . 2. Composers—California—Hollywood
(Los Angeles)—Biography. I. Title.
ML422.P82A3   1991
780'.92—dc20
[B]   91-19733
CIP
MN

ISBN 0-385-41341-6

10 9 8 7 6 5 4 3 2 1

This book is for my wife Heather.

It was her idea to have me write down some of these stories, and once I was committed to doing so, it was she who saw to it that I was disciplined enough to finish them. She then did me the loving favor of laughing loudly when she read the finished product, an act of affection and approval which I will not forget.

I would also like to thank Jacqueline Kennedy Onassis, who edited the book, and whose unerring judgment was probably tempered by her enjoyment of slightly wicked stories.

Prologue

THESE RAMSHACKLE REMINISCENCES of mine are of a particular period in my life, a period that came to a permanent close twenty-five years ago. Since then my life has become totally different, my work, my ambitions, my outlook all so removed from those days long ago as to make them seem vaguely unreal. For sixteen years, from 1948 to 1964, I worked in Hollywood as a film composer, arranger, and conductor. For most of those years I was under contract to MGM, the largest studio in the world, and quite an education it was.

Although I was unaware of it then, those were the final days of true excess, a time when every film made money, when the stars were above and beyond normal criticism. Premieres were right out of Nathanael West, executives were ferocious tyrants, and way way down the list, seated well below the salt, were the writers and musicians, a beaten lot, whining and bitching about everyone else's illiteracy. Of course our behavior was mostly predicated by guilt; there had been no Torquemada to make us renounce Art and opt for hard cash and soft shirts; that had been a set of private decisions.

I used to soothe myself with the reminder that my decision had been tempered by necessities; I had to make a living, I had to help my family, and I did continue to study and learn serious music during the time I spent fashioning harp glissandos for Esther Williams's high dives. But actually, these are all cop-outs, lame excuses. I was eighteen years old when I signed my contract at MGM, and suddenly, there within my grasp, was all the tawdry glamour I longed for. I was making quite a bit of money, the work was not seriously daunting, my coworkers were generous and kind, and the chorus girls gleaming in the California sun fit easily into my blue convertible. Who could resist, who would want to? Certainly not I, not yet, not then. Let's face it, I had fun. It was terrific. My responsibilities were few, the thought of advancing years had not yet reached me, I was good at my job and had lots of time left over for reading, studying, or conversely, tennis and the good life.

Now, with the clarity of hindsight, I realize that I was in the last gasp of the Hollywood that is held in such nostalgic reverence today. Students of the cinema tend to be more serious about the films of Raoul Walsh than any group of music conservatory inmates preparing their Ph.D. thesis on the madrigal since Gesualdo. I worked on a great many of the MGM musicals—with Gene Kelly, Comden and Green, Astaire, Garland, Vincente Minnelli, and Alan Lerner. It never occurred to any of us that we might be working on anything that would last; we were simply putting together something that, with any kind of luck, would turn out to be entertaining. The era I lived through in Hollywood is utterly gone and will never happen again. I doubt that anyone really mourns its demise; it was pretty awful. But I suppose it is worse now, and so the mishaps and mistakes of the past have taken on a kind of glowing patina. But I shouldn't, and mustn't, make comments on today's movie world. I don't know about it and I don't live in it. My memories are of a simpler time, when the studio was the plantation, and we all worked in the fields. It may not have been admirable but it was clear-cut and, in an elusive way, pure.

No Minor Chords

ONE

THE FIRST DAY I reported to work at MGM, I arrived by bus. To be precise, two buses. The year was 1946, I was sixteen years old and not quite yet finished with high school, and I was about to become a member of an honorable, highly skilled, and faceless army known as The Arrangers and Orchestrators, whose job it was to take the sketches or piano parts devised by the studio's contract composers and turn them into organized orchestral music.

At three o'clock the bells signifying the end of a normal school day rang and I was off at a dead run in order to catch the 3:10 bus a block away. I made it with at least three seconds to spare and spent the ensuing fifteen minutes trying to get my breath, buttoning my flapping sweater and jamming books and loose papers into the kind of string bag beloved by Rumanian ladies shopping for cabbage. This first bus was a fairly up-market vehicle; it was red and sleek and barreled through Beverly Hills at a respectable clip. When it reached the corner of Burton Way and Robertson Boulevard, I got off and waited for the second bus, a decidedly poorer relation. This one was green and square and rattled alarmingly. The seats were made of some kind of revolting imitation leather, long gashed and torn, and invariably there would be someone in a two-tone "loafer" jacket reading Mickey Spillane. It went very slowly and was given to stops that had no reference to passengers either getting on or off; I think it was simply that the bus was exhausted and had chest pains.

After an interminable ride it turned into Culver Boulevard, a street boasting the highest number of motels in California as well as countless fast-food stands advertising such delectable fare as Chick-enfurters and Giant Tamales. It was into this bleak environment that I got off in order to walk down a side street and to arrive at Metro-Goldwyn-Mayer Studios.

The firm's slogan in those days was "More Stars Than There Are in Heaven," but they certainly weren't in evidence from my initial vantage point. The first entrances I came across were adorned with large iron turnstiles and looked as if they were the gates to a city jail. There, the "extras" of the day were herded through and checked off, all those nameless, mute faces in photographed crowds, ready to report to the wardrobe department and be fitted out with the correct Indian headdresses or Roman togas. I was grateful to pass up this particular tunnel into the studio, but it took me quite a while, that first day, to realize that the main gate was on the street behind this facade.

Once I found that small avenue, I saw the view that was to greet me every day for the next twelve years: on one side of the road was a giant parking lot ringed by huge advertising placards heralding the current MGM product. "Laughter, Tears, and Brawling Action— Wallace Beery as *The Mighty McGurk*" was one; another sign announced shyly: "One of the most stirring stories of the decade— James Craig and Butch Jenkins in *Boys' Ranch.*" Across the road from this display of understatement were two white buildings: the small one on the corner was a mortuary, privately owned and independent of the studio, although God knows enough jokes were made about it, and a very large edifice, the Irving Thalberg Building, which housed the powerful members of the MGM clan—the executives, producers, and directors—as well as the subterranean projection rooms, the executives' gym, the offices of Louis B. Mayer, and down a smallish corridor the working quarters of a few top writers. Most of the doors were imposing in an uneasy melding of Tudor and Biedermeier conceits, but all of them had in common a nameplate that could be changed in a matter of seconds.

I had no quarrel with any of this when I first saw it. In fact, I was crazy about it and considered myself extremely lucky to be there. Looking at the Irving Thalberg Building, and admiring its thirties facade, I turned to my right and found myself looking into the drive-in gates of the studio itself. These gates were closely watched and guarded. No one drove or walked in without being checked and identified by the uniformed gateman, a gentleman named—no, I'm not making this up—Kenneth Hollywood. Whether the name came before the job, or the job before the name, remained a mystery throughout my dozen years in the place, but surely no Restoration play ever boasted a more directly named personage.

When I arrived, he checked his list of the day and found that I had indeed an appointment with one of the studio's composers, Georgie Stoll, and I was waved through with the instruction that I should report to the music library first, to fill out a few papers.

All the music department bungalows were clumped together, on a street to the left of the main thoroughfare. These little houses were truly dilapidated, with banging screen doors and peeling paint, but to my sixteen-year-old eye they all resembled Le Petit Trianon. I found the music library. It consisted of many huge, high-ceilinged rooms, all filled with every note ever written for the studio. Songs, scores, arrangements, utility music, Academy Award efforts, and football marches, all in the manuscripts of the composers. I subsequently spent countless hours idly going through these drawers and coming up with really fascinating musical relics, all irreplaceable. A couple of decades later, a new studio chief, James Aubrey, ordered all the music in the MGM library burned, in order to make some extra space. Tons of score paper were incinerated, all covered with penciled notes—hours, weeks, months, years of effort thrown away. In the rooms immediately beyond these vaults were the copyists' offices. In 1946 there must have been at least twenty copyists under contract, each of them working all day long, just to keep up with the ceaseless flow of new music being handed in. Presiding over this was Arthur Berg, one of the three chief librarians.

"You hand in all your work to me," he said. "I'll get it copied, make out your union bill, and then you can get paid."

He was a man then in his sixties, with the kind of immaculate white hair that usually goes with Florida car salesmen. He had the sort of reddish baby complexion that looks as if he had never found it necessary to shave. I was in awe of him that first day, figuring that the keeper of such archives would be a walking Grove's Dictionary of Music. I was wrong about that. He liked to compose, from time to time, not movie music, but little, anachronistic piano pieces, usually called "Album Leaves" or "Dance of the Elves," suitable for display on the music rack of upright pianos. While I was filling in the employment forms Arthur handed me, I sneaked a look at the roster of the music department, nailed to the wall. The contract composers were Miklós Rózsa, Herbert Stothart, Bronislaw Kaper, Lennie Hayton, Georgie Stoll, Scott Bradley, David Snell, Adolph Deutsch, and David Raksin. I knew all about them. I could recite all their credits. I was not anywhere near being able to join their company, but I was very pleased to be in the same place. My reverie was interrupted by the entrance of another librarian, Jules Megeff. Jules was relaxed and always seemed slightly amused. He introduced himself to me and asked what I was supposed to be doing at the studio. I told him.

"Well, well," he said, smiling. "So you're another little helper for Georgie! You'll have an interesting time. Let me tell you how to get to his office; it's not easy."

I thanked him and paid attention to his set of directions. He followed me to the door. "Have you ever worked for anyone before?" he asked. "What I mean is, you're kind of young, have you orchestrated for anyone before?"

I felt it was time to assert myself, and I told him of my days at the Paris Conservatory, and of my musical studies since. Jules's face betrayed nothing of his thoughts; he would have been a perfect John Le Carré hero.

"Paris Conservatory, eh?" he mused. "Well, good luck, kid. And listen"—and his voice became just a trifle conspiratorial—"don't be taken aback by Georgie. He's a little—unusual."

Georgie Stoll was quite an apparition, with hair like the woolliest of the Three Stooges, and clothes he could have found only by diligently combing the thrift shops of the Bowery. He drove an ancient Duesenberg and lived in a house that would have inspired Bram Stoker. He was also sweet-natured and kind and never hurt anyone. I must confess that I never actually saw him write anything, and I don't know whether a genuine Georgie Stoll Urtext manuscript exists anywhere, but he always had a keen nose for the talented newcomer, and dozens of Hollywood's best arrangers went through his particular school. There are many people who play the piano with just one finger, but Georgie was the only one I ever met who played with just his thumbs. It was very weird, but you got used to it. He would stand at the piano—he was too restless to sit —and sing and bang his thumbs and shriek and explain, and somehow some kind of mysterious message got through and you would go home and write something that was undeniably based on his singing and banging and shrieking, and it would work quite well in the film.

As far as his ability to read music was concerned, well, he was an ex-fiddler, so treble clef held no fears for him, but the rest was the Dead Sea Scrolls to him, most particularly the transpositions that are necessary to any orchestral music. To the uninitiated, a page of orchestral score must look as hopeless as a page of calculus looks to me. When it came to the recording of the music, Georgie would always conduct from a sort of simplified piano part, while the orchestrator who had actually put all those dots on paper would sit, unobtrusively, near the podium and field any questions that might arise from within the ranks of the orchestra itself.

One day this caused a problem. The music we were recording had been written partly by me, and to a greater extent by a remarkable French arranger called Leo Arnaud. Leo had listened to a rehearsal of the sequence he had written, and there had been no mistakes or problems. Leo thought it was a safe time to go to the bathroom, so he disappeared, taking his scores with him.

Almost immediately one of the trumpet players had a question.

"Georgie," he called out, "what's my second note in bar 37?"

Georgie looked around for Leo. No Leo. He knew I was of no use, since I hadn't written the piece in question. He panicked and stalled for time.

"Would you run that sequence again, please, I want to check something," he shouted at the projectionist. I sensed impending disaster and went off at a trot to find Leo. I found him down the street, in the Gents, sitting in contented privacy. I explained the situation hurriedly.

"Mon dieu!" said Leo, coming out of the door at a dead run. We burst back onto the recording stage in time to hear the aggrieved voice of the trumpet player.

"Jesus, Georgie, what do you mean I'm wasting everybody's time, I just want to know what's my second note in bar 37?"

At this point Leo was flailing through his manuscript pages with one hand, and trying to hold up his unbuttoned pants with the other.

"F sharp," he suddenly yelled. "Ralph, you should have an F sharp!"

Ralph shot Leo a grateful look, but he knew the rules of the game as well as we did.

"Thank you, Georgie," he said, and the recording resumed.

BUT I AM getting ahead of the plot—for what was I doing at MGM in the first place?

My father, a successful lawyer in Berlin, knew just about every corner of the European continent. He was widely traveled, but his journeys never took him across the Atlantic Ocean. Therefore, his knowledge of the United States was based on a few letters from fairly distant relatives in New York, from novels such as Dreiser's *An American Tragedy,* and from films about the Pony Express. When it became inevitable that the family would, if allowed, move to America, it was only natural that his thoughts were firmly anchored in New York City. However, one day he arrived home in deep thought. He had gone to the movies and had seen Loretta Young in *Ramona,* that hoary old story of Helen Hunt Jackson's. This was one of the earlier, garish Technicolor efforts, and in terms of artistic accomplishment it ranked with the bottom ten on anyone's list. But it contained a scene that had made a deep and lasting impression on my German father.

"Imagine," he told us, "the whole family had breakfast on a veranda, outdoors. Red strawberries! White milk! Bright sunshine! Green lawns! Let's try to emigrate to California!"

None of us were knowledgeable enough to advise him as to whether the visions of Darryl Zanuck had any basis in reality or not. All we knew was that since we were bound to leave, it might as well be that a California terminus was all to the good. We managed to leave Germany on the pretext of having a weekend in Paris, which meant that my parents took absolutely nothing with them. My father's library, the furniture, paintings, crystal, the piano—it all had to appear as though we were coming back. The plane landing in Paris must have been the most extraordinary catharsis imaginable—to all but me, wrapped in the callousness of childhood and convinced that it was all wonderfully exciting.

Six months went by in Paris. I managed to be accepted as a student by the organist and composer Marcel Dupré in the conservatory. We lived in a street behind the Madeleine, in a hotel much more accustomed to renting rooms by the hour than to housing a refugee family. At last our visa came, delivered by a friend from Switzerland, and we piled onto the *S.S. Manhattan,* landing in New York in November 1938. We were met and welcomed by my father's second cousin and his wife, as well as by their twenty-year-old son Homer. Homer took one look at me, in my very German knickerbockers and cap, and took pity on me. He and I went in a separate taxi, and on the way to his parents' apartment he showed me what the New York skyscrapers looked like, and topped this miracle off by inviting me to my first exposure to an American ice cream soda. Of course I drank it much too fast, and the excitement, mingled with the weird mixture of soda water and ice cream, made me instantly ill. I showed my gratitude to my new relative by throwing up all over the drug store and my shoes.

My father's determination to match Loretta Young's breakfast was undiminished. He had another second cousin in Los Angeles, Charles Previn, who was a music director at Universal Studios. This tenuous link to family was all the encouragement we needed, and we all duly arrived in Los Angeles, looking for a temporary home, a way to earn some money, and four portions of strawberries in the sun.

My father's lack of English and the fact that he could not pass the California Bar Exam explained our alarming lack of funds. He had always been a very good amateur pianist—his enthusiasm compensating for lack of technique—and he soon became the neighborhood piano teacher, a job where his German accent was a decided asset rather than a liability. I was, like most ten-year-olds, fairly heartless, and I thought it all a great adventure. Not until many years later did I realize that my father must have led a life of some considerable despair and disappointment, and that his courage in keeping us afloat was extraordinary. He wasn't the only member of the family at odds with the language. I did not speak a single solitary word of English. My biggest regret at the time was that I could not read anything but German, and that my favorite books, Mark Twain and *Bulfinch's Mythology,* were a hopeless task in their original language. Suddenly I was reduced to feeling great pride in actually mastering a page of Donald Duck. My father hit upon an idea somewhat akin to throwing a child in a pool in order to teach it to swim: he enrolled me in a perfectly normal grammar school, figuring, quite correctly, that with the receptivity of childhood I would pick up the language a lot quicker that way than I might with a tutor and a set of grammatical primers.

To supplement this idea, he told me to go to the movies often, making sure that I saw the same film several times in a row. It is actually a terrific way to pick up a language and its colloquialisms. At the time of our arrival in Los Angeles, we lived in an apartment hotel called the Palacio, on Sycamore Avenue, off Hollywood Boulevard. It has always struck me as endearing that the sleazier the hotel, the grander the name tends to be. There are more flea bags called Le Royale, or the Prince George, or the Palatial Arms than there are those with more modestly apt names. At any rate, around the corner from the Palacio was a famous cinema called Grauman's Chinese, and the price of a ticket for a child under twelve was a dime.

I liked going to the movies and enjoyed the fact that a totally inexplicable plot became slightly more graspable when viewed for the fourth or fifth time. I remember a few of the films I saw that first month: a comedy with the Ritz Brothers; a Wallace Beery film that tutored me in how to say "Aw, shucks." *Trade Winds* baffled me. Decades later I spoke to Fredric March about my confusion with that film and was given the following explanation. It seems that both he and his leading lady played twins, and the complications ensuing from two people acting like four and being baffled by it themselves were obviously a bit much for a German child trying to pick up the odd phrase or two. March laughed a lot at the thought and then confided that he had never quite been able to follow the plot himself, even while he was filming it.

As a whole, my father's idea worked pretty well, and I was able to master more and more English. It's a good thing I learned from the movies in their 1939–40 state of censorship. Had it been today's films, my early efforts at conversation would have sounded like the badinage of members of the shore patrol.

School was more difficult for a while. Every time anyone spoke to me, whether it was a teacher unaware of my problem, or another pupil, I would nod and smile vacuously, completely in the dark. They must have thought I had an IQ of minus ten. However, there were some kind souls who took me under their wings, and I learned soon enough.

All in all, I had a totally straightforward childhood: Selma Avenue Grammar School and Beverly Hills High School, a clapped-out old rattletrap for a car in my senior year, and the school dances. My attendance at these proms was fairly regular, not because I took my girl dancing, but because I had the band. Occasionally I would try my hand at writing arrangements; more often I would go to the local music shop and buy band arrangements for two dollars each, a practice now forgotten with the demise of dance bands, but very popular in my youth.

I suppose what made my life in high school different was the simple fact that I played the piano quite well, and that I had enough musical curiosity to try various kinds of employment. After school, twice a week, I played the piano at a dancing school on La Brea Avenue, making up tunes and banging them out while hapless and enraged teenagers learned the *soi-disant* etiquette that was supposed to go with dancing. That job ended when the school's proprietor, a Mr. Swarthout, insisted that I play a song called "Blueberry Hill" for an entire hour, after which I left, catatonic with boredom.

There was another after-school job, more interesting, but also unfortunately short-lived. At that time, there was a small movie house on Highland Avenue called the Rhapsody Theatre, which ran only silent films for a cult audience or for those who thought them hilarious. I was hired by this theater to sit in the pit and improvise piano music while the movies unreeled—in other words, in imitation of the only music the movies knew before sound. I was paid a dollar an hour and had a great time making up melodramatic music, Western chases, Keystone Cops funny music, and whatever. I certainly didn't know it at the time, but this engagement was a harbinger of things to come. The occasion when I booted that job was simple but in the best farce tradition. The film in question was epic in length and kept switching back and forth between biblical times and the Roaring Twenties, flappers and allegories akimbo.

I was watching the screen—I never saw the films before I improvised to them—and playing properly quasireligious nonsense when suddenly the story slammed into a different gear and madcap flaming youth were Charlestoning like crazy and imbibing bubbly from silver slippers. I thought, with logic on my side, that the images would stay in this mold for a while, so I enthusiastically modulated into a manic version of "Tiger Rag," both hands flying. After less than a minute the audience was giggling and I looked up to see the manager storming down the aisle, his face quite alarmingly contorted. I shot a glance at the screen, but it was much too late; I had been caught in a montage and was pumping out "Tiger Rag" as an accompaniment to the Last Supper. I think my employment ceased before I could play the next cadence. It was not to be the last time a movie score of mine was thrown out.

When I was sixteen years old, I began to write an arrangement or two for radio shows. There was a local effort called California Melodies, one tune for the Fanny Brice show, and a truly deadly weekly half-hour with Hoagy Carmichael and a band simply known as The Teenage Band. These stumbling efforts of mine led to an unexpected offer. MGM was then engaged in making endless musicals, many of them featuring the pianist José Iturbi. Mr. Iturbi had had a fine career, he had even assayed a Mozart concerto with Toscanini, but he had, of late, succumbed to the lure of money and indolence and had agreed to play "himself" in these films. Usually he was seated at a piano, preferably a white piano with a mirror on it, by the side of a swimming pool, either practicing Tchaikovsky while Esther Williams swam in smiling circles, or accompanying Judy Garland in what was misnamed "boogie-woogie." Now the studio felt it was time to play less arcane selections and it was suggested that he try some "jazz" variations on "Three Blind Mice," to the edification of the listening Jane Powell. Iturbi was a very accomplished pianist, obviously, but jazz or any derivation of it was Egyptian hieroglyphics to him. Someone at MGM, mysteriously enough, had heard of "this kid who plays jazz and can write!" and, sensing cheap employment, sent for me.

GEORGIE STOLL'S OFFICE could be found only by negotiating endless back alleys and deserted streets, and on that first day it took me a long time before I could find his lair without the feeling of triumph one has after emerging from the Hampton Court maze. Then there were two flights of outdoor, iron stairs without bannisters—the kind where you expected Fu Manchu upstairs, or at the least, an illegal doctor. Finally, at the top, there was Georgie's place. (I should add at this point that "Georgie" was not a diminutive address of affection but the name he went by and under which he worked. "Johnny" Green was another musician whose credits on films were listed thus. Many years later his appellation suddenly became not "John," but John W., driven, I suppose, by a somewhat tardy desire to appear more distinguished.)

Georgie's offices can only be described as filthy. Not the kind of Bohemian, intellectual garret-filth, but the dirt and neglect of a disused hotel in the lesser neighborhoods of Buffalo. The carpet was torn and stained, the piano scarred and burnt and so desperately out of tune as to make it the object of derision in a whorehouse. There were production schedules of movies that had been made ten years earlier Scotch-taped to the walls, and his desk was the only one I have ever seen in my life that had ants on it.

Georgie was the music director of the Iturbi film in question. He had been a mainstay of the MGM music department for many years, had been music director of all the Judy Garland–Mickey Rooney extravaganzas, and had even won an Academy Award for his work on *Anchors Aweigh*. He was married to a charming blond girl with blurred features whose name was Dallas. He drove Gary Cooper's 1934 Duesenberg, and lived in a house that was a cross between the motel in *Psycho* and Gloria Swanson's abode in *Sunset Boulevard*. Under all these layers of eccentricity lived a very nice and gentle fellow. He told me what was wanted of Mr. Iturbi, banged his thumbs on the piano for occasional illustration, and sent me home, this time on three buses. That night I did my homework for school and then wrote out the "Three Blind Mice" variations; they weren't long, and certainly not complicated. The next day, same routine. School, two buses, labrynthine alleys, Georgie Stoll. He was perfectly pleasant, but confused.

"Wasn't my explanation clear yesterday?" he asked. "What is it you need to know?"

"Nothing, Mr. Stoll, I'm finished, here's the music."

He thought I was kidding. "You wrote that in one night?"

I wish I could now take credit for some Herculean task, some manifestation of genius, but to tell the truth it had been easy, and it would have been easy for anyone with reasonable facility. Georgie paid me compliments which were quite out of line, and then told me to give my music to his staff arranger-orchestrator so that an orchestral accompaniment could be devised for the movie. I took courage, based on the incredulity I had seemingly caused by my speed, and asked, "May I do the orchestration myself? It would be easier, and you can always throw it out if it's no good." Georgie laughed, gave his assent, and my tenure at MGM began.

Several times a week I would make my after-school pilgrimage and ask whether there was any need for my services. Often there was, at first mainly for Georgie, but then for a few others. I wrote football marches for a short subject, orchestrated a sequence or two for harried and hurried composers of "B" pictures, played the piano for a Tom and Jerry cartoon, and generally made myself useful.

Had I been paid by the job, at union prices, I would have made quite a bit of money; as it was, the powers of the music department were too smart for that. Within a month of my first visit, I was offered a contract; certainly modest, but a contract, a real live commitment from a real live movie studio. I was given an all-inclusive weekly salary of $125, for which I did everything but park cars. I loved it and was grateful for the chance, as well I should have been.

Now that the late late shows are fond of disinterring ancient movies, I have on occasion seen forgotten horrors from the late 1940s boasting my youthful work, and I have genuinely shuddered at my presumption and have felt like hiding under the nearest sofa. And yet the studio was neither a philanthropic place nor a school for budding composers, so at the time, they must have thought my work adequate for their purposes. My new contract came with a catch. They wanted me to finish my high school years at the studio school, a small sunny building between the cartoon department and Rehearsal Hall C. In this variant of the classic, one-room American schoolhouse were all the child actors of the day—Elizabeth Taylor, Jane Powell, Darryl Hickman, and many other talented or benighted, cute or repellent, famous or hopeful children, all of different ages and interests, all finishing their minimum, state-required daily dose of schooling. I have no idea why I suddenly came to my senses or how I came to have the necessary fortitude to say no, but no is what I said, loud and clear. I went back to my sensible high school and figured I would see enough of studio life after I had graduated in the accepted manner.

But my work continued, at first sporadic and then more and more regularly. I soon found out, coached by my friends the arrangers and orchestrators, that the only musical job totally controlled by union fees and not covered by weekly stipends was actual orchestrating. The musicians' union decreed that a page of orchestration was to consist of four bars, that payment was to be made by the page, and that, therefore, each four bars was worth whatever the traffic might bear over and above the minimum, which was of course what I worked for. The brilliant musician Leo Arnaud, whom I mentioned earlier, was also deciphering Georgie Stoll's thumb melodies; he was French, had studied in Paris, and knew everything worth knowing about the orchestra. He became my benefactor, unofficial teacher, advisor in how to write for the harp, and my Baedeker to the Rules of the Game.

"Listen, *mon vieux,* " he confided one day. "When you are orchestrating for a true musical illiterate, then it is perfectly okay to take advantage of that situation here. We don't get any credit, so the idea is to make as much money as possible. When I am asked by one of our innocents to ghost-write some chase music, for Western posses or gangland car rides, the music has to be very fast, eh? Well, write the meter in 3/8. This means that"—and he sang a demonstration—"bubbidy bubbidy bubbidy bubbidy, two seconds of music, is already a page, whereas a more normal 4/4 or 12/8 bar would only take up a quarter of a page with the same notes. Mind you," he continued, "this must only be done with those employers of ours who can hardly read music. With the good ones, it would be dishonest."

These were interesting lessons in variable morality for a teenager.

More important, I was getting a thorough schooling in the practical aspects of music making. Nothing teaches as much as experience, and I was surrounded by talented people who were willing to be helpful. I learned how to orchestrate quickly. I have, in recent years, received some compliments on being a good and supple accompanist to my soloists. The reason for that, in my opinion, goes back to my studio work of the late forties and fifties. I had to conduct for a lot of unorthodox, or to put it more bluntly, unmusical singers, and once a conductor has learned to cope with the vagaries of musical naiveté, none of the occasional waywardnesses of genuine musicians is a problem.

Best of all, and most important of all, I was privileged—later on —to stand up in front of an orchestra of superlative players countless times, probably several times a week for ten years, rehearse them in brand new music, make the necessary changes, and record it, all as quickly as possible without sacrificing the performance. I learned how much an orchestra can be put through, what makes them tired or angry or irritable, and what pleases them. All orchestral players, whether at MGM or in the Berlin Philharmonic, like to get on with it: don't waste a lot of time, don't talk too much, and have a conductor firmly in charge without being arrogant or self-aggrandizing. Only a few months ago I watched a young conductor in front of the Vienna Philharmonic for the first time. He was frightened of them, which is totally understandable. At one point in the rehearsal the principal violinist asked about a bowing at a certain place. Should they start the phrase upbow or downbow? The young conductor wanted to ingratiate himself with this august body of players. "Well," he said winningly, "what would you like?"

And from the back of the viola section came the answer. "What would we like? Well, a decision would be nice!"

All this I learned in, of all places, Culver City and Burbank. It would have been nice to be a *répétiteur* in an opera house in Wiesbaden and learn all those things while in the service of immortal music instead of in the service of Kathryn Grayson, but learn it I did, and at an early age. When I composed, I heard my music played by the orchestra within days of completion of the score. No master at a conservatory, no matter how revered, can teach as much by verbal criticism as can a cold and analytical hearing of one's own music being played. I would mentally tick the results as they came at me: that was pretty good, you can use that device again, that was awful, too thick, that mixture makes the woodwinds disappear, those trills are not effective, that's a good balance, and so on and on. I paid very close attention and tried to be reasonably ruthless with myself.

QUITE APART from all these laudable and educational reasons, it was a practical necessity that I earn some money. My older brother Steve was working, of course, but in a family as uprooted as mine it was more than welcome to have both sons contributing to the budget. My father was by now established as a piano teacher, but his pupils were very much of the "nice little girls should play the piano" variety, and they drove him mad. Often I would be in the kitchen of our small house, aware of the frightful hacking on the piano emanating from the sitting room where he was giving a lesson. My father would suddenly appear in the doorway, utter a heartfelt "Oh God," and disappear again.

Poor man; he loved music so very much. His musical predilections, however, were tried-and-true conservative German. Every new piece was compared to Beethoven or Schubert, unfavorably to be sure, and modern music stopped with Richard Strauss. I attended a concert at which I had my first hearing of the Bartók Concerto for Orchestra, and came home in a white heat of enthusiasm. I talked so incessantly about it that my father finally agreed to go to the repeat performance two days later and take me with him. We sat in the auditorium, listening, and I was as knocked out as I had been before. Bartók's piece came to its smashing end, and my father turned to me, lips thin with disapproval. "Well," he said, "it's not the *Eroica!!*"

I must have ground my teeth with frustration; it was pointless to insist that it wasn't *meant* to compare with, or displace, Beethoven's Third Symphony; in my father's view, if it didn't measure up to the *Eroica,* it was decidedly second-rate. About twenty-five years later I found myself conducting a series of concerts devoted to the works of Oliver Messiaen, the extraordinary French composer, whose music is not exactly meant to soothe. At the end of the lengthy symphony there was polite applause from the notoriously conservative audience, a few boos from the back, and a steady stream of people clawing their way up the aisle in unseemly haste. The next night, before I began the piece, I told the audience the story of my father's reaction to Bartók. They enjoyed the story and laughed and applauded. And then, at the end of the Messiaen, we got what I would call a crouching ovation; not quite a standing one, but near enough. By the way, the intervening twenty years have made the Bartók concerto sound tame and beautiful; its ability to shock has long been superseded by newer and more violent musical expressions.

WHEN I THINK, from my present vantage point, to some of the demands made on musicians at MGM, I cringe in retrospect. For example, early on I worked for a composer named Herbert Stothart. He had been an operetta composer in the twenties and had achieved a firm foothold at MGM, with his name on most of that studio's heavy dramas. Hardly a tear was shed on screen for better than twenty years without Herbert Stothart's accompanying music. His method was to devise pretty themes and melodies which were then turned over to one of the musical drones for metamorphosis into something orchestrally usable. I was assigned to concoct the title music to an "important" epic, and Stothart had been explicit in his instructions to me. He handed me his tune, which was very nice indeed, and said "Big! Big! Impressive! Use a huge orchestra! Add a chorus if you want to. Or an organ. Or extra brass. Big!!"

By this time stoic acceptance had become second nature to me. I went to my office and wrote sort of an anthology of effective bad taste; the ending of "Pines of Rome" was modest by comparison. On the day of the recording, Mr. Stothart was on the podium, his gestures reeking with authority, his head leonine. At a respectful distance behind him were the producer and director, in attitudes of awe and admiration, pilgrim students at the feet of Beethoven. I was sitting, as invisible as possible, on the bottom step of the conductor's rostrum, following my score. As the music headed for yet another fortissimo wallow of excess, Stothart leaned down toward me without missing a beat.

"Young man," he stage-whispered, "did I write this?"

But I loved the studio, I loved the way it smelled, I was crazy about Indians in the lunchroom, and Romans making phone calls, and the highly charged and technically dazzling music making on the recording stage. Most of all I loved being a part of it, a part of a peculiar fraternity, belittled and superior at the same time, envied for all the wrong reasons and commiserated with for the stuff we all took in our stride. Within months of my arrival at MGM I was witness to conferences that had some fairly bizarre dialogue.

One of my earliest film assignments was *Big City,* starring Margaret O'Brien and Danny Thomas. The producer was Joe Pasternak. He was phenomenally successful at purveying the commercial cornball musical, as opposed to the much more highbrow Arthur Freed product. Joe liked Kathryn Grayson's tremulous singing, Esther Williams's flawlessly stiffened hair, and Mario Lanza's alarming voice, which brooked no musical dynamic under an eyeball-rolling triple *forte.* His stories were formula, the songs mostly by Hungarian friends, and you couldn't find a subtext with a Geiger counter. Joe was wonderfully candid about all this, and very happy with his pictures.

"No one ever gets sick in my scripts," he said accurately and proudly. By the way, this was an attitude shared by other producers. When Walt Disney decided to film a life of Beethoven, he felt that deafness was too downbeat and not really germane to the story, so for once, and in glorious Technicolor, Beethoven retained perfect hearing to the end. Classical music has generally been a closed book to the movie executive mind—witness this meeting in Pasternak's office held to discuss a possible song for the great German soprano Lotte Lehmann to sing in *Big City.* What the greatest Marschallin in *Der Rosenkavalier* was doing in this mess to begin with is beside the point. I was playing through various suggestions for repertoire when Miss Lehmann shyly offered the opinion that the Brahms "Lullaby" might be suitable.

"Well, sure, of course, I take that for granted," shouted Joe. "After all, you made that song famous!"

Six years later, Joe called me one day and reminded me that for story reasons in the film *Small Town Girl,* the hero and heroine, Farley Granger and Jane Powell, had to attend a chamber music concert. Joe wanted me to record something in the public domain, meaning that there was no fee for copyright, and this something had to include a piano, again for plot reasons.

"Remind me, will you," he asked cheerfully, "I forgot. A string quartet is a harp and what else?"

I managed a straight and civil answer, and decided to record the first movement of the Schumann quintet with the four string principals of the MGM orchestra. We had a lovely time playing it (it was rather unusual repertoire for Culver City), and once the record had been cut, I sent a copy of it to Joe for approval. It was not long in forthcoming. His voice on the phone was filled with enthusiasm. "Hey, that's a great piece, kid; it's so terrific that I want to use more of it than I originally planned. But since I like it so much, I want you to record it again, and this time with a full orchestra." I thought he was kidding. No, he wasn't.

I tried pointing out that the word "quintet" has certain inalienable meanings, both in music and in language, and that I couldn't really change Schumann.

"What are you talking about?" The voice was getting less amiable. "If it sounds good with those four schleppers it'll sound a thousand times as good with a whole orchestra. Now go and do it." I waged a quick battle with myself and decided to be a puny hero. I refused to do it, and Joe took me off the picture and had me put on suspension.

Kathryn Grayson's husband, Johnny Johnston, had a habit that made Joe extremely nervous. If someone told of a highly successful round of golf, Johnny would quietly contribute that he had managed one stroke less on the same course. If it was mentioned that someone had bought a Bentley, Johnny would say that he owned a Rolls. When hearing that a new pool had been put in at someone's house, he said that he had just done the same, but his pool also had a waterfall. In short, no matter what the subject was, great or trivial, Johnny had gone one better. This rankled Joe fiercely. One day, on the recording stage, Johnny had gone through the usual one-upmanship litany, and Joe's patience ran out. He went and stood facing Johnny from a distance of no more than two inches, and yelled at him, "This morning, when I got up, I took twenty-seven showers!!"

·   ·   ·   ·

EARLY ON I HAD a memorable encounter with the boss of the studio, L. B. Mayer. He was a short, plump, and unimpressive-looking man who would wander through the studio streets surrounded by a phalanx of blue-suited Uriah Heeps. He would bestow a kindly pat on the head of a child actor as he passed, and wave regally and absentmindedly to the producers and relatives thronging the street. His office was amazing; it was huge and it was white. And when I say white, I mean white. No hospital corridor, no novitiate's robes were ever whiter. The carpet, the walls, the ceilings, desk, chairs, sofas, and lighting fixtures were all snowy and pristine, a kind of Las Vegas home for runaway vestal virgins. Here Mr. Mayer would sit, his feet not quite touching the floor, and make decisions that shaped the American Dream for more than two decades. His opinions were unassailable.

One afternoon I was scheduled to play the piano at a charity party given at Pickfair, the palatial home of Mary Pickford and Douglas Fairbanks, and Mr. Mayer, seeing me make my way to the parking lot, had his limousine stop and very kindly offered me a ride. In the vast car with him were two minions: one was a man named Lester something-or-other whose job consisted of agreeing with his boss with such microsecond alacrity that he kept a handkerchief balled in one hand to wipe the foam of eager assent off his lips. The other gentleman was always seated at Mr. Mayer's table in his private dining room (to which invitations were highly prized) and he would make sure, many times during the period of a luncheon, that a box of the boss's favorite matzohs was easily to hand. Therefore, he was known to one and all as "Triple M," Mayer's Matzo Mover, and no one ever figured out what else he did.

Anyway, I digress. There I was eighteen years old, on the jump seat of the limo, totally out of my depth. Luckily, L.B. started the conversation.

"Did any of you gentlemen go to the Hollywood Bowl last night?"

For once I was the only one nodding. It had been a remarkable concert of Jascha Heifetz. "What was that weird thing he played, do you happen to know the name of it?"

I couldn't figure out what it was that had seemed weird to Mr. Mayer. Heifetz had played the Sibelius Violin Concerto with his usual perfection and ardor. I started to speak, but Mr. Mayer cut across my feeble attempt. "No, you can't possibly know, nobody's ever heard of that thing before, he shouldn't play pieces no one's ever heard of, it's ridiculous. Anyway, that's one of the reasons he's not a success."

He's not a success? Who's not a success? Heifetz? I was trying to get my breath, Lester was bobbing and nodding, and Triple M was looking for matzohs. It actually wasn't until some years later that I worked it out. The equation was actually quite simple: Heifetz was not in the movies. Ergo, Heifetz was not a success.

On that same car ride to Pickfair, Lester studied the somewhat overcast sky. "I sure hope it doesn't rain, L.B., and spoil the garden party," he offered. Mayer looked out the window briefly, then said in a dark voice, "They wouldn't dare."

I never figured out who "they" were.

With Hedda Hopper, and deeply embarrassed.

My fellow escapee from the sound stages Miklós Rózsa, conducting a rehearsal in 1952. I have no idea what we were playing, but at least it didn't have dialogue over it.

On the set with Vic Damone and Nat Cole. As is obvious, I always admired Nat's piano playing.

A meeting of the Screen Composers Association, 1952. Sir William Walton, Lyn Murray, unidentified, Bernard Herrmann, and me. I don't know the lady in the foreground.

Fritz Loewe and Alan Lerner look on while Louis Jourdan proves
to me that he reads music fluently.

My first Oscar, being handed to me by June Allyson and Dick Powell.

My old friend Gene Kelly has just handed me my Oscar for *Porgy and Bess*.

Billy Wilder, Mike Nichols, myself, and Adolph Green, singing *Threepenny Opera* loudly, if not well.

With Frank Capp and Red Mitchell at a recording date. We look unnecessarily serious.

The Subterraneans was an unintentionally risible film, graced by some great jazz players. Here are Bill Perkins and Gerry Mulligan.

Moonlighting in a jazz club with Shelly Manne and Red Mitchell.

Remember "Poetry and Jazz," an early sixties concert? Russ Freeman was at the second piano, but he ducked out of the frame, the clever man.

I am obviously exhilarated by Isaac Stern's virtuosity while he is obviously exhausted by it.

TWO

IT DIDN'T TAKE LONG for my work at MGM to become more interesting. One day I had a phone call from a producer called Robert Sisk. He had originally been a member of the Theatre Guild in New York and was now producing well-made, harmless movies. He was a particularly nice and intelligent man with a passion for collecting first editions, and his desk was always piled high with delectable catalogs from forthcoming book auctions. At any rate, he offered me my very first film to compose, one where I would be given the credit and the responsibility would be all mine. I was over the moon, grateful and excited. I almost didn't ask what the project was to be. When I was informed of the particulars, it didn't faze me at all, although in retrospect, the contributing factions seem weird enough to be part of a game, played by vindictively hip participants.

The story was called *The Sun Comes Up*, script by Marjorie Kinnan Rawlings, who had written the successful and sensitive novel *The Yearling;* the director was Richard Thorpe, a workman of the old school who always brought in his assignments ahead of schedule and under budget; and the stars (in order of their billing!) were Lassie, Jeanette MacDonald (her last film), and Lloyd Nolan. The story was pure insanity, some sort of goulash involving a world-famous soprano driven to seclusion in the Ozark Mountains by the loss of her child, and the subsequent renewal of her faith, her high C, and her love of mankind, all by way of the wise ministrations of Lassie.

Robert Sisk made an additional contribution to my status at the studio, and it was one that needs an explanation. The initial struggle for anyone working in the film industry is to get credit on the screen, no matter how small or tucked away one's name might be. I had had a few such credits, as arranger or pianist, but you had to look very quickly to see them. The final goal was always that piece of ephemera known the "separate card," by which is meant a moment in the credits where your name, and your name alone, fills the screen. It is considered the final accolade, and writers, composers, and designers kill for it. Well, Bob Sisk, as a surprise to me, gave me such a separate card, and there, at the preview of the film, I saw it, my name, in Technicolor, "Music by André Previn," filling the screen, and my eighteen-year-old heart was suffused with pleasure.

What did I care that it wasn't Dostoyevski? It was my own movie, my name was on it, and besides it was tailor-made for music, since the dialogue was sparse in favor of a lot of barking in picturesque meadows. Miss MacDonald sang two songs (Fauré and Puccini), and although her voice always had been a bit peculiar, she was the soul of kindness, she worked hard, and I liked her a lot. The film was a success, by which is meant that it wasn't an abject failure, and suddenly I was given new assignments as a full-fledged film composer.

My second job was a good, tough melodrama called *Border Incident,* about the criminal treatment given illegal Mexican labor, smuggled across the border into Texas. I never saw the finished movie, but I think it was exciting, and to the point. I wrote an angry-sounding and occasionally dissonant score and won the praise of some of my colleagues. Then, in appallingly rapid succession, came about six more films, all within two years, most of which have mercifully receded into the fog of oblivion. One of them was a cops-and-robbers story about a police precinct in Brooklyn. The day after I first saw it I was called into the office of the producer, a gentleman named Nicky Nayfack. I believe he was a distant relation of L. B. Mayer's. Nicky had a request pertaining to the score. "I want you to use the song 'Cielito Lindo' as the main theme, kid," he commanded. My brain seized up. "Cielito Lindo" is a sentimental Mexican folk song. This film took place in Brooklyn, with tough-talking detectives, sneering criminals, and available hat-check girls. Had I missed some subtle subsurface dimension? Was there an allegory to be hammered home? I was completely at sea. I was nineteen years old and incapable of saying "What the hell are you talking about?" and I didn't want to lose the assignment. I said something moronic like "Let me think about that," and sneaked back to my office.

I most certainly did think about it, for the rest of that day and for most of the night. In the morning I gave up and went back to Mr. Nayfack. I admitted my confusion, reminded him of my lack of experience, and begged for an explanation.

"No big deal, kid," he said, making sweeping gestures. " 'Cielito Lindo' happens to be my favorite song and I want a record of it to play at home."

I didn't use the song, I didn't work for Nicky again, I struck up a warm friendship with the hat-check girl, and the film self-destructed soon after its release.

It goes without saying that being a young man under contract to the world's biggest studio had a great many compensations, not the least of which was the fact that many of the prettiest girls in America floated down the streets in a never ending stream. I enjoyed myself thoroughly, but there is one occasion which I should describe in detail. I had just come to MGM a few months before, I was seventeen years old, and my lack of sophistication, no, make that innocence, no, make that stupidity, was all-encompassing. Teenage was a different kettle of fish then; censorship still existed, and not every film in distribution tried to rival the Kama Sutra in explicitness. I had gone to a party where there were a lot of people, and the usual amount of noise. I was sitting at the piano, casually noodling some pretty Rodgers and Hart, Kern, and Gershwin, when Ava Gardner sat down on the bench next to me. Ava had arrived at MGM a scant two years earlier, and she was the kind of beautiful that turned men into Jell-O molds. She listened to me play, quite attentively, and then asked an incredible question: "Would you like to take me home later?"

Well, I was seventeen and I simply could not allow myself to put a subtext connotation to this, so I asked, "You mean you don't have a ride home?" Ava gave me a long, searching look, saw that I was serious, excused herself, and got up from the piano bench.

Now let's jump ahead two years. I was nineteen and considerably hipper in the ways of the world. There was another party and again I was playing the piano. Ava was there, although not anywhere near the piano bench this time. I finished playing and strolled over to her. She gave me a friendly, if cool, hello, and I decided to prove my recently found confidence. "Can I take you home later, Ava?" I asked blithely. She gave me a radiant smile of pure sweetness, and patted my hand. "Go fuck yourself, kid," she said, and that is the end of my Ava Gardner story.

AMONG THE ESTABLISHED STARS I met as a kid, Errol Flynn was irresistible. We met while I was writing an expendable score to an adaptation of Kipling's *Kim*. The plot called for Flynn to sing a short song, and when I went to teach it to him, I found that he was almost totally tone-deaf. He couldn't even approximate the correct notes. I told him not to worry and that I would get a vocal double for him, not an unusual dodge. Errol's eyes lit up as he thought of a fine practical joke.

The producer of the film, Leon Gordon, was a gentleman much given to ascots, public school accents, and references to India. Errol thought him a thorough fraud. Gordon had made his name by writing and producing a risible turkey called *White Cargo*, in which the Viennese Hedy Lamarr, covered with Nestlé's cocoa powder, plays a native girl who announces to a hapless British planter, "Me, Tondelayo. Me, bad girl. Me stay with you." Anyway, Errol devised quite a plan. I went to the recording stage with an excellent baritone named Bill Lee, and accompanying him on the piano, we committed the song in question to film. Then I called Leon Gordon and told him that unbeknownst to all of us, Flynn actually had a wonderful singing voice, and that I would send the test recording up to his office. Leon heard the song and instantly rushed to Flynn's dressing room. "It's wonderful, just great, you're a really fine singer. How is it that you've never made a musical?" Errol looked shy and said that no one had ever asked him. "But that's ridiculous, you'd be a smash! Here at MGM they make the best musicals ever, would you do one for us?" Flynn said he was a bit hesitant, but if Leon would go to L. B. Mayer and tell him what a good singer he was, then perhaps something could develop.

"Absolutely," replied the beaming producer, tugging his scarf into place, "L.B. has great faith in my judgment." And off he went. Duly, Mayer appeared in Errol's dressing room and relayed the news that Leon Gordon had raved about his singing voice. Oh, said Flynn, he didn't really think he sang that well. Mayer was adamant. "Leon said that in his opinion you could be a great musical leading man." Finally, practically fluttering his eyelashes, Errol agreed to sing for Mayer, and proceeded to fill the room with his tuneless braying. Mayer was aghast; that goddamned idiot Gordon! He murmured some excuse and ran off, presumably to scream at the bewildered producer. Errol was in seventh heaven; the gag had worked perfectly, just as he had imagined it. He thanked me profusely. "I won't forget this," he said.

Around eleven that night I was sitting in my small apartment in Westwood, reading, when the doorbell rang. I couldn't imagine who it could be. When I opened the front door, there was Errol, beaming and not what you might call cold sober. He waved at me and said, "Hi, I've come to thank you and to bring you a present." He pushed an extremely pretty Chinese girl through the door and, before I could gather my wits, ran down the stairs and disappeared. I doubt that he would ever have become a disciple of women's rights or a favorite of Betty Friedan's. Of course his values needed some revisions, and he was a thorough rogue, but it was very difficult not to like him.

MOST OF MY WORK around those early days was involved with totally nonsensical, utterly forgotten films. In the meantime, I certainly did not entirely neglect my serious studies. Although my conducting was autodidactic and would remain so until two years later (1952), I played a lot of piano and took part in a great many local chamber music evenings. There was a quite prestigious series called the Monday Evening Concerts, for which I performed regularly. The repertoire at these concerts was an ingenious mixture of old and new, established and experimental, and I was willing to try anything. One of the most gifted film composers ever, David Raksin, has remained a good friend for thirty years, and he recently found and sent me some programs from those evenings. It was a fairly astonishing list; I had taken part in performances of works by

Boris Blacher, Beethoven, Mozart, André Jolivet, Rolf Lieber-
mann, Bach, and Stravinsky. There is one crystal-clear remem-
brance: I received a call from the founder and director of the concerts, Lawrence Morton, who informed me that they had had a
very unfortunate series of cancellations for the following week, and
would I consider playing the Mozart Two-Piano Sonata in D together with Lukas Foss?

I didn't think I could. "I've never played it, Lawrence," I demurred. "It's a difficult piece and we won't have much rehearsal
time." Oh, that's okay, he reassured me. Lukas had played the piece
innumerable times and would guide me through it easily. It's a
gorgeous sonata, you'll have fun, it will really help us out, and so
on and on. Of course I felt good about the flattering invitation, so
I agreed. A quick phone call to Lukas Foss set up a time to read it
through at his house (he was the one with the two pianos at home)
and I did some exploratory practicing. When I arrived at Lukas's
house, we chatted for a while, he told me about his new composition, and then we tentatively sat down at the two Steinways. I was
apologetic. "I don't know this piece," I confessed. "Never played it
before. Thank goodness you're an old hand at it, I need help."
Lukas leapt to his feet and his voice rose in pitch about a perfect
fourth. *"You've* never played it? What are you talking about? *I've*
never played it but was told you knew all about it!"

There was a minute's silence while we digested the fact that we
had fallen for one of the oldest con games of the entrepreneurial
world, and then we both began to laugh.

"What the hell," Lukas said, "we've got two whole days, all the
time in the world, let's start." And start we did, *tabulae rasae,* but
with enthusiasm.

There is a postscript to this small story: The morning after the
performance, the *Los Angeles Times* carried a review in which it was
noted that it had been a pleasure for the critic to hear a performance so carefully studied and prepared and thought-out. Well, it
only proves a maxim I have tried hard to remember: It is perfectly
correct to disregard all the bad reviews one gets, but only if at the
same time, one disregards the good ones as well.

A few weeks later, I played the Stravinsky Piano Serenade in the
same series of concerts. When I walked out on stage, I saw, sitting

in the first row, Stravinsky himself, and at his side, Aldous Huxley. It was roughly as though Mount Rushmore had suddenly been placed into the auditorium. I played in a sweat. Applause. I went backstage. The door opened and Stravinsky came over to me. I was very young, and totally devoid of speech. The great man gazed at me, his face expressionless, and then he uttered only one sentence: "You have wonderful fingers." With that, he left, stranding me in an enigmatic fog. Was it a compliment? Was it damning? I didn't know then, and I certainly don't want to know now, thirty years later.

It wasn't long after this that I was taken to Arnold Schoenberg's house. California, at that time, was teeming with the great men removed from Europe by the war. Stravinsky, Schoenberg, Rachmaninoff, Thomas Mann, Bruno Walter, Lion Feuchtwanger, they were all there. No one of them seemed a less likely Californian than Schoenberg, the forbidding personage who had invented serial music, the twelve-tone system. It may be true that kids do not yet go off to school whistling his themes, but it is completely beyond cavil that he was one of the seminal figures in twentieth-century music. I was taken to meet him by George Tremblay, a composer of Schoenbergian disciplines and his former pupil. The walk from the great man's gate up to his front door was enlivened by a huge dog jumping and tearing at the chain that affixed him to the wall. The dog seemed close to insanity in his rage and frustration, and he would have been much more apropos on the moors surrounding Baskerville Hall than on the tranquil manicured lawns of Southern California. Perhaps the animal had been trying to teach his master's system to some unwilling pupils, and had finally snapped under the pressure.

Schoenberg himself was a lot less frightening, at least physically. He was kind to me, and actually seemed interested in my musical development. He gave me a short theme and asked me to improvise on it at the piano, something I knew I could bring off with some degree of proficiency, and he was more than complimentary. He then questioned me on a few theoretical and technical matters, and my answers were not as fluent as they might have been. He gave me a list of books to read, and suggested certain works for me to study. I was grateful for the advice, but more than that, amazed that I was actually standing with, and talking to, Arnold Schoenberg. It was a hot day and we went outside for lemonade. To my surprise, there was a Ping-Pong table in evidence, and to my even greater surprise, I was invited to have a game with Schoenberg. I was relieved that the musical part of the meeting was over, and I played happily. I was callow and young and inexperienced, and I beat the old gentleman. It was a dumb move, and the composer of *Gurre-Lieder* was not pleased. I left soon after, and the howlings and ravings of the slavering hound behind me were a good reminder for me to be just a bit more thoughtful in the future.

About that time I had a meeting with another towering musical emigré from Europe. The great violinist Joseph Szigeti maintained a residence in a suburb of Los Angeles called Palos Verdes. He was one of the handful of acknowledged masters of the violin, and a man passionate about finding and playing new works. His reputation as a champion of modern music was well known throughout the world, and aspiring composers were in the habit of sending him their recent manuscripts, in the hopes he might find their brainchildren attractive. The pile of untried new music on his piano grew, and he mentioned to an old friend of his, Willem Vandenberg, that he needed a pianist to help him plow through these works. Willem was a fine cellist who split his time between the most serious work imaginable and moonlighting in the film studio orchestras. He was short, bustling, high-voiced, and he chain-smoked vile little cigars. He also seemed to know everybody, and he now mentioned to Szigeti that at MGM Studios there was a young man who was purportedly one hell of a sight reader. Should he call him? Szigeti agreed, and so I received one of the most surprising and unexpected phone calls of my life.

Again, the innocence—and arrogance—of youth prevailed, and I enthusiastically agreed to go to the fabled violinist's house the following Monday evening. I wasn't even experienced enough, or smart enough, to be frightened. I was certainly aware that I had some very long shortcomings, but I did feel reasonably sure of my sight reading. Szigeti was friendly and courteous, and he put several handwritten manuscripts in front of me; I had never heard of the composers and I had the feeling that they were the lesser avant-gardists of Bulgaria. Anyway, I did my best to acquit myself without total shame, and after about an hour, we took a break. Szigeti smiled and made a suggestion. "That was rather hard work. Willy is here tonight, he has his cello in the car. Let's relax from all that dissonance and play a Beethoven trio. Which one do you want to play, André?"

Now, at last, I had the grace to be embarrassed. "It doesn't matter to me, Mr. Szigeti, I've never played any of them."

Szigeti looked at me with the kind of bewildered interest one summons up when looking at an unidentified substance under a microscope. Finally he spoke, and he chose his words carefully.

"That's disgusting," he said. "Unforgivable. How can you play the piano like that and not know the Beethoven trios? Here's what you are going to do. You are going to come back every Monday evening and we'll start going through them, beginning with Opus 1, Number 1, and we'll also play Schubert and Brahms until you have some semblance of a civilized chamber music repertoire. And during those evenings, we can also play through some of the new stuff I've been sent."

He was as good as his word, this kind and generous man. I went back for many evenings. What he didn't know about chamber music wasn't worth knowing. My adoration for this particular kind of music making has remained steadfast and unwavering all through my life, and I will always be grateful to him. Shortly afterward, I formed a trio, together with the violinist Israel Baker and the cellist Edgar Lustgarten. We called ourselves the Pacific Art Trio and played concerts up and down the West Coast, for anybody who wanted us. We were all involved in film studio work, and this endeavor was a sort of life raft for the three of us. It was far from unusual for us to work throughout the day on a Tom and Jerry cartoon and then meet after supper to prepare the Ravel trio.

One time we were planning a performance of the Shostakovich trio, fairly new at the time. We had the typical chamber music discussion (otherwise known as a screaming argument) about the tempo of the first movement. The printed metronome markings in the score seemed arbitrary to us, and none of us believed them. I had an idea. "Let's call Shostakovich," I offered. My two colleagues laughed. "Where?" asked Eddie. "Do you happen to have his phone number?"

A few more scathing remarks back and forth, and I got on the phone in Eddie's split-level Van Nuys living room and asked for Moscow Information. It took endless time and some surreal dialogue, but I was finally put through to an English-speaking member of the League of Composers in Russia. I explained who we were and what our problem was, and by God, we were given an appointed time twenty-four hours later to put through the call, at which time an interpreter would be on an extension. So there I was the next day, with a flushed face, inquiring about metronome markings and being answered by Shostakovich, by way of an interpreter.

I must now explain to the nonmusician that the tempos of a composition are designated in the music by metronome markings which consist of notes of varying lengths followed by a number of two or three digits. These numbers when set onto the metronome cause the instrument to make a clicking noise in the desired speed of the music in question. Also, the letters of the alphabet are used to make stopping and starting in a long work easier to find, the letters being distributed throughout the printed work. Therefore, my conversation to Moscow went something like this: "At seventeen after A, does a quarter equal 132?"

Answer: "No no, that's wrong, read eighth not quarter, and eleven later, just before B, it should change to half equals 60."

My two trio companions were listening to all this and excitedly taking notes, when suddenly Iz Baker began to laugh uncontrollably. I waved at him in a fury, but he finally had to leave the room. When my monumental phone call came to an end, I asked him, in icy tones, just what he found so amusing.

"Think about it," he gasped. "The whole town is seething with the activities of the House Un-American Activities Committee, everybody's afraid to give any kind of opinion, obviously a phone call to Moscow is monitored by the FBI or somebody, and they will most certainly think you were talking some sort of code!"

It didn't take Eddie and me long before we were as enamored of the situation as Israel had been. I had happy visions of Senator McCarthy being given the new metronome markings of the Shostakovich Trio and trying to manufacture a sinister plot to overthrow Van Nuys out of it. At the time nothing official ensued.

Nearly a decade later I was working on *Porgy and Bess* for Sam Goldwyn.

McCarthyism's hold on the public's paranoia had lost some of its grip, but Hollywood was still submissive to such arbiters of patriotism, defenders of morals and deciders of careers such as Ward Bond, Ginger Rogers's mother, and Adolphe Menjou. The climate was still truly creepy, and just about the only safe discussion in the studio commissary was about the salads on the menu, and even then you had to be careful about Russian dressing. One day, the daily gossip column of the *Hollywood Reporter* carried an item that stated that it was a disgrace that André Previn allowed so many Pinkos to play in his film studio orchestra. That same day I was summoned to Sam Goldwyn's office. Goldwyn was sad, but he wanted to remind me that at MGM those musicians who had been accused of being fellow travelers had been dismissed so summarily that they had been prevented from coming onto the lot in order to clear their instrument lockers of their possessions.

I took a deep breath and assured Mr. Goldwyn that I was quite certain that the musicians in the *Porgy and Bess* orchestra were neither Communists nor Fascists, they were just musicians. I told him that they were much too busy playing music to pass out pamphlets, that the criterion of their having been hired had been the fact that they were the best people available, and that I would give him my word that the playing of the orchestra would not subvert the audience into attempts to overthrow the government. Goldwyn thought about it. Then he said, okay, he believed me. However, he went on, if any one single member of the orchestra ever turned out to have questionable politics, I would be fired the same day.

A few weeks later, a letter came, requesting that I come to the offices of a gentleman who was running a small, private magazine dedicated to the "exposure" of Hollywood Reds. Armed with total ignorance, I showed up at the man's desk at the appointed time. He gave me hardly a glance but shuffled through a stack of papers in front of him, his face positively radiant with booze. Finally, he leaned back, envisioning himself as the Burbank Inquisitor, and said, "I have certain information that you gave benefit concerts for the Abraham Lincoln Brigade during the Spanish Civil War. What do you have to say to that?"

I was almost sorry that my answer was so simple. I reminded him that although I had sometimes been on the receiving end of the flattery that I had been precociously talented, I could not take credit for concerts in 1936, since (1) I was six years old when the war began, and (2) was living in Berlin.

It was so obviously the unadorned truth that even my inquisitor recognized it as such. He thought about it. Then he stood up and grasped my hand across the desk. His hand was very warm, and so wet that I thought a large animal had licked my palm. He smiled and chuckled. "No harm in trying, eh?" he asked. He was, for a while, a feared personage in Hollywood; then he went to prison for blackmail.

I DOUBT that there has ever been an interpretive musical artist as venerated as Jascha Heifetz. One would have to go back through history, for the likes of Liszt or Paganini, to approximate such adulation. Any violinist anywhere, when asked about Heifetz, gets dreamy-eyed and starts stuttering in his search for the adequate vocabulary. The particular blend of passion, complete perfection of technique, intensity, and beauty of sound remains unchallenged. All of Heifetz's records are reissued periodically, whenever a new wrinkle in records makes its mark—78, LP, tape, CD—and they are always spectacularly received. His current counterpart, Itzhak Perlman, has collected every available or pirated snippet of Heifetz's playing, and one time played a tape for me, made from an ancient radio broadcast, of a duet played by Heifetz and Jack Benny. "Listen to that," he said, entranced in front of the speakers, as the alternating phrases of "Love in Bloom" wafted through the room, "Listen how perfect, how beautiful, how effortless, oh God!"

Heifetz was a close friend of my parents, particularly my mother, and periodically he would call and invite us to come over. I heard the most amazing chamber music in his Frank Lloyd Wright–designed studio. Piatigorsky, Emmanuel Bay, Israel Baker, Virginia Majeski, William Primrose—they all played. Unlike at Szigeti's house, I was not there to play, and I wonder if I would have had the nerve anyway. I was more than content to sit and listen; participants in chamber music tend to lose track of time, so these evenings of music would go on and on, for hours on end, and I was in seventh heaven.

It must be admitted that once Mr. Heifetz put down the fiddle, he was a considerably less Godlike figure. For one thing he was tough on his kids. The radio was on one evening, the broadcast of a concert, and Mozart's 40th Symphony was being played. One of the Heifetz children came in, in order to say hello to the guests. Heifetz asked, "What's the name of the piece they're playing?" When the child professed ignorance, she was summarily sent out of the room. "My children should know the Mozart G Minor," he said, unforgiving.

He was misanthropic by nature and, in his later years, a recluse, seeing no one and suspicious of everyone who tried to get in touch with him, including his old friends. He must have been deeply unhappy once his concert days were over. He taught for a while, and I witnessed a master class at the University of Southern California. A young female student had been playing the Bach Chaconne for him, and he had criticized the sound she was producing. "Let me show you," he said, and played a few bars so beautifully as to make one's head swim. The girl was overcome. "Of course, Mr. Heifetz," she stammered, "but it has to be admitted that I'm playing on a kind of cigar box, and you have your Stradivarius." Heifetz's response was wordless. He took the student's cheap instrument, tucked in under his chin, and proceded to play for several minutes. The sound he was making was the same as the one he had produced on his own violin. He finished, handed the fiddle back to the girl, and unsmiling, uttered the one word: "So?"

The most bizarre example of his hydra-headedness was on display one afternoon when he invited a few friends over for an auction. This needs some elaboration. During his ceaseless travels, he had been the recipient of a great many presents and accumulations, and every few years he would then auction them off to a carefully selected room full of acquaintances. He would open the door to his house, wearing a battered top hat, and exclaim, as words of welcome, "Hello, suckers!" Once a bid from the assemblage had been accepted, he would bang a gavel and enter the amount into a large ledger. Obviously he derived huge pleasure from all this, and his smiles were nothing short of radiant. I have vivid memories of a couple of extraordinary instances: Among the items to be auctioned, there were, of course, wonderful things: pictures, rare books, masks, tapestries, and cuff links. But mixed in were old razors, discarded clothes, and other inexplicable goodies. Heifetz had very small feet, and during one auction, when he brought out a large carton containing some two-dozen pairs of unwanted shoes, there were no bidders, no takers. Akim Tamiroff, the Russian character actor, was suddenly revolted. "Why don't you send them to a charity, Jascha, the Salvation Army or something?"

Heifetz was undeterrable. "You want to send them, by all means," he said. "What'll you bid?"

Tamiroff, out to embarrass, offered fifty cents per pair. "Great," shouted Heifetz, down came the gavel, and the shoes were sold.

During a break in the proceedings, a gentleman walked up to Heifetz's manager, who had successfully bid for, and bought, a beautiful wrist watch. "What did you pay for it?" the man asked. "One hundred dollars," said the manager. "Let me give you two hundred for it," was the offer. "No, no, please," was the answer, "I'm already embarrassed by the fact that I bought it. If you like it so much, give me the hundred I spent on it and take it."

"You mustn't feel bad about my offering you two hundred," said the man. "Last Christmas I gave it to Jascha for a present, and it cost me five hundred bucks."

During all this, Heifetz stood facing his guests. Behind him was a sort of alcove filled with books and records ready to be auctioned, and I was riffling through them. I noticed that from time to time the door to the kitchen would open, and his cook would peer out, unseen by the guests in the living room but visible to me. Somewhere during the afternoon, an elaborate and beautiful scale model of the Heifetz sailboat, the *Serenade,* was brought out. "How about this item?" announced Heifetz. "Great for somebody's kid!"

The kitchen door came half open, and the cook peered out. "Mr. Heifetz, excuse me, but if you would remember, that's the boat I thought I could get for my nephew."

"Okay, what's your bid?"

There was understandable indecision, and finally the cook murmured, "Ten dollars."

Heifetz turned to his guests, who had not been witness to this last exchange. "How about you, Franz?" Heifetz turned his attention to the film composer Franz Waxman. "Wouldn't your son love this?"

Waxman smiled. "Yes, I guess he would. Okay, twenty-five dollars."

Heifetz turned to the kitchen door. "Well?" he asked.

The cook made a negative gesture. "I'm so sorry, Mr. Heifetz, I can't afford that."

"Right," said Heifetz cheerfully, turned back to his guests, banged the gavel, and said, "Sold to you, Franz, for twenty-five dollars."

It was all a bit much for a teenager to digest, much less to understand or view philosophically. A good analyst would have had a ball, and would have come up with interesting theories and reasons, but I was way out of my depth. I managed to buy a very handsome wooden music stand, which I still own, but when I was leaving and saying goodbye to the host, he stopped me.

"Are you giving any concerts next season?" he asked.

I mumbled that they weren't anything within light-years of his concept of a concert tour, but yes, I did have about a dozen appearances planned.

"I have a lot of extra evening clothes," he said, "and we're close to the same size; I bet my tails would fit you. Shall we try?"

I was touched and nodded assent. He fetched the suit from upstairs and made me try on the coat. He was right, it fitted almost perfectly.

Heifetz beamed. "You see?" he said. "It's terrific. How much will you give me for it?"

I stuttered that I didn't know. "How about, oh, let's say twenty dollars?" he asked. I was the color of tomato aspic, made some kind of *sotto voce* noise, dug in my pockets, and gave Jascha Heifetz twenty dollars.

Even with hindsight and with experience of the passing years, I can't explain this particular aberration by so great a musician. How could a man play the Brahms Concerto so that involuntary tears would be shed by listeners all over the world, and turn around and conduct these auctions? On reflection, though, it must be said that there are a great many legendary names from the past whose accomplishments and personal predilections did not match. I wouldn't have wanted to go on a walking tour with Gauguin, and Wagner would not have been a great babysitter. What Heifetz did on the violin was, is, and will be untouchable, crystalline, and perfect.

THREE

MY FIRST BIG ASSIGNMENT as a music director at MGM was a Fred Astaire musical called *Three Little Words,* the life story of the songwriting team Kalmar and Ruby. It was a big movie, some fairly long dance numbers needed to be composed, and it was certainly the most important break I had been given at the studio. Working with Astaire was a complete joy. Much has been written about his perfectionism, and he truly was unsparing of himself, dancing tirelessly in the studio rehearsal rooms and discussing endless details pertaining to his numbers. He was friendly and adored gossip; not the malicious kind, but just silly chorus-line gossip. He liked playing the piano, and he was a good drummer. His effortless elegance made everybody around him look like Dumbo, and I had a wonderful time working out his music with him.

Fred certainly was not as easy to know as Gene Kelly. He was extremely private, and was not given to making casual social engagements on the spur of the moment. I most certainly don't want to give the impression that he was not friendly or funny, but away from the studio he tended to keep to himself. It was difficult to pay him a compliment; he had been an icon for so long that it was almost an impossibility to find the right words. Curiously enough, he was very diffident about his singing. He had put together, at his home, a film library of all his dance numbers, but all of them had been shorn of the vocal that precedes the dances. He seemed to be oblivious of the fact that he was many musicians' favorite singer, or if he knew it, he was embarrassed by that fact. The fact is, of course, that his consummate way with a lyric, and his particular, airy, rhythmic voice prompted the greatest American songwriters to write very specifically for his style of presenting popular songs. Fred probably found it difficult to identify with anything removed from dance. When *Three Little Words* was finished, I asked him to sign something for me—a photo, an album, the inside of a match book, for all I cared. He waved me away, smiling but vehement. "No no," he said, "I can't do that." But two days later, a studio messenger brought me one of Fred's black, formal canes, with which he danced when wearing top hat and tails. Approximately two inches of the ebony wood had been scraped away meticulously so that the natural, light color underneath was exposed. He had written "To André from Fred" on this surface. It would have been a lot easier, physically, for him to write his name on a photograph, but it was a lot more natural for him to sign a piece of dance memorabilia.

The songwriter Harry Ruby, whose exploits were the basis of *Three Little Words,* was around, and was endlessly amusing. He had a witty, craggy face—someone described him as looking like a dis-honest Abe Lincoln. He was another man who lusted for first edi-tions, and on Saturdays I would meet him at a small antiquarian bookshop on Santa Monica Boulevard owned by an erudite, soft-spoken man called Max Hunley, whose eyebrows flew off the sides of his face. There we would sit, in front of an ever-going small fire, Max's protest against the California heat outside, and see if we could afford the tiny shop's latest acquisitions. I bought some Joyce, a lot of Huxley and Fitzgerald, while Harry grew feverish over early editions of Twain. As an end-of-picture present, he gave me Henry Major Tomlinson's *The Sea and the Jungle,* and Max Beerbohm's *Zuleika Dobson.* He was also a walking encyclopedia of baseball and the possessor of a wonderful sense of humor. One day, in the MGM lunchroom, he and I were seated at the writers' table, a long rectangle reserved for whoever was writing scripts at the time. Suddenly a man rushed into the canteen, causing quite a commotion, and headed over to our table.

"You'll never believe this, fellows," he practically babbled, "they've just fired Sam Katz!!"

Sam Katz was one of the biggest executives at MGM, and had

been for decades. It was unthinkable, like the Eiffel Tower being dismantled.

"Fired!! Sam Katz fired?"

"Yup, you heard me," said the bringer of the bulletin. "They bought him off by giving him his salary for the remaining years of his contract, they advanced his pension, they gave him another stock option, and a bonus of a million dollars. And then they fired him, just like that!"

The table thought about it in silence. And then Harry Ruby banged his fist down so hard that the glasses jangled. "Well, that'll show the son of a bitch," he said.

Astaire's co-star in *Three Little Words* was Red Skelton as Bert Kalmar. He was the one who always had to play the piano on camera, so I was sent to his house to find out whether he could play at all. I was ushered into Red's sitting room, and there he was, facing me from behind a large-sized grand piano, playing like mad.

"Hi," he called, "just let me finish this," and the notes continued to cascade forth with consummate ease and expertise. I was astonished and happy. "Pretty good, eh?" he asked, and when I nodded my respect, he suddenly got up and walked away from the keyboard. The sounds continued unabated; Red owned an elaborate player piano and had set the moment up with perfect timing. When he saw my face, he laughed his infectious child's laugh and was in a completely happy mood. I think he told the story as often as I did.

Three Little Words was a happy experience for me. The finished film was pleasant and mild, and it made money. Quite a lot of work came my way because of it, but first I had to overcome a sudden jolting halt in my life: at the age of twenty, I was called into the army for two years.

I SUPPOSE a word of explanation is necessary at this point. In 1950, the year in which I went into the army, the Korean War was being waged, and although the word "war" was not officially used, a great many young men in the reserves and in the National Guard suddenly found themselves in barracks. I had joined the National Guard on the advice of my father, who reckoned that this was a dandy way to avoid being drafted. I spent a couple of desultory Tuesday evenings in a Los Angeles armory, being taught what "turn left" meant, and then was blithely notified that my unit had been mobilized into the regular army, beginning the following week.

Korea seemed an incomprehensible fact, but in the years between World War II and Vietnam it simply never occurred to young men to scuttle to Canada or burn their draft cards. I must admit that, had I thought of these extreme measures, I probably would have embraced them; however, they weren't within our ken at the time, so I found myself standing in a railroad siding at five in the morning one day, having been given a farewell lunch at MGM studios 24 hours earlier. The reaction of my colleagues there had been one of disbelief rather than dismay, and the teenage Elizabeth Taylor had giggled and said, "You're kidding," a sentiment wholly justified in my opinion.

At any rate, there I was, lined up, freezing, and being shouted at, when the melodramatic thought occurred to me that I was finally going to pay for the easy life, for my professional precocity, for the pretty girls and the open cars. It turned out that I was premature in my pessimism; I was never sent overseas and I was never shot at. However, this was not because anyone took an inordinate interest in my welfare; it was just the turn of events.

Basic training was in a spa called Camp Cooke. Places like it have been described in print since Gutenberg stumbled onto movable type, so I will content myself with saying that it was thoroughly loathsome and depressing, two requisites for any army camp. On the first morning, we were assembled in front of the barracks before dawn. As luck would have it, I was standing next to a very good jazz bass player called Don Mills, an extremely pleasant man, suitably thin and unkempt. Our commanding officer, a lieutenant in a uniform so new that it squeaked when he walked, paced between our ranks. He sported cavalry boots shined to an alarming sheen, and he actually carried a riding crop. His gaze fell on Don, and his military mien clouded over. "You need a haircut, solider," he barked. Don smiled ingratiatingly and said, "Yeah, I'm hip." This was ill advised. The officer stared, doubting his hearing. *"What?"* he shouted. Don was perplexed but sanguine. "Okay, I'll get one, right," he offered. This was a heaven-sent opportunity for the shiny lieutenant.

"You'll get one *what?"* prompting the missing appellation "sir."

"I'll get one haircut, isn't that what you wanted, man?"

"What you wanted *what?*"

Don grew a mite restive. "I said, like, I'll get a haircut, man, I got to wait until the shops open!" He then turned to me and said in a conversational tone, "Do you know what's the matter with this guy, what's he want?"

I said, "He wants you to call him 'sir,' " which made Don laugh, which made me laugh, which made the assembled grotty gathering laugh. One hour later Don and I were in the kitchen, scouring pots and peeling potatoes. My army record has nothing very notable in it but I feel reasonably certain that not too many draftees were put on KP within the first hour of life in uniform.

The officer in question, our budding Patton, 2nd Lieutenant Caruso, lived his fantasy to the fullest. A helmet liner precariously perched on his head, a webbed belt for the ammunition so necessary near Lompoc, California, that riding crop swishing about, he was the complete military man, striking authoritative terror into our collective souls. We thought him a product of West Point and a student of Clausewitz's *On War,* and he made our lives thoroughly miserable. One night, halfway through basic training, I had drawn the assignment to sit all night in our Company HQ, in order to answer any phone calls or to sound the alarm in case of marauding enemy platoons. I wrote some letters and soon grew bored. There was a cabinet with all our histories neatly filed in it. Idly, I looked through a few, and there was our military genius: Caruso, Joseph, 2nd Lieutenant. I scanned his background. Oh, how wonderful life sometimes is! Our officer, so battle-scarred and combat-weary, had been, until a few weeks earlier, a Good Humor man. Just in case you have forgotten, the Good Humor man was an American institution, an ice cream vendor in a slow van, who inched his way through suburbia jangling little tuned bells which played the first four bars of "The Band Played On" over and over again. My eyes raced over his *curriculum vitae* and I found that his base of operations had been Culver City, California, home of Metro-Goldwyn-Mayer. It was too good to be true. Had I actually bought Raspberry Twistees and Eskimo Pies from him while his little cart was parked in front of the studio?

The next morning I wasted no time in imparting the happy news to our company. We lined up for inspection. The lieutenant walked with weighty steps between the ranks. From somewhere in the back came a soft, sweet tenor voice, raised in song: "Casey would waltz with the strawberry blonde . . ."

Caruso's head whipped around. "Who did that?"

Silence. The pacing inspection continued. From someplace else came, ". . . and the band played on . . ."

The lieutenant stopped dead in his tracks. The nerve had been hit. "Stop that, stop that singing," he hissed, then wheeled and started up the barracks steps.

This time, humming followed him, in fact, humming in harmony. "Casey would waltz with the . . ." at which point the doors slammed and he disappeared.

Lieutenant Caruso was not the same after that. He had a slightly hunted look about him, and soft melodious whistling answered most of his commands. Not long after, he was transferred, probably at his request, to our regret and his relief.

Obviously, my life at the studio receded more and more, until a quite unexpected moment reminded me of it. Along with about a dozen men, I was engaged in that most enjoyable army duty, the digging of a latrine trench, when a jeep drove by and a corporal screamed, "Previn, report to the Orderly Room right away." I was baffled but secure in temporary innocence, brushed off the worst of the mud, and trotted off. In the Orderly Room I marched up to the desk and saluted the officer on duty. He barely looked up. "There's a telegram for you, Private," he said. "You've been nominated for an Academy Award or something." He handed me the wire. There it was, courtesy of Western Union; I had indeed been nominated for an Oscar, for my work on *Three Little Words*.

There was no time-honored reaction possible. I stood, filthy and silent, and the officer said, "That's all, dismissed," and I turned around and marched out. I got back to my duty and jumped into the hole we were digging. My friend Joe Russo wiped off some sweat and leaned on his shovel.

"What took you away from this uplifting line of work?" he asked.

"I'll tell you later," I said, and then finally I began to laugh, so much that I had to sit down on the ground. Of course I didn't know it at the time, but it was to be the first of fourteen such nominations, but the only one where I can still recall the exact circumstances of my finding out the news.

Around this time, with basic training mercifully close to ending, someone at headquarters took a look at my file and decided that I might be worth sending to the Film Unit of the Signal Corps to write music for their training movies. I was made aware of this possibility, and while the musical lure of composing apt back-grounds for *How to Assemble an M1 Rifle* or *How to Avoid VD on Furlough* seemed minuscule, the thought of receiving a direct commission and living in Washington, D.C., was not to be sneezed at.

I was therefore pursuing this assignment with alacrity when the assignment officer, quite as an unimportant afterthought, hit me with the news that a direct commission involved a minimum of three years from the date of acceptance, instead of the remainder of the two years for which I had been inducted. Never has it been so easy to turn down an offer; I asked for the assignment to be given to someone else and decided to take my chances for a shorter pe-riod of time.

I was shipped, for a time, to the Proving Ground in Provo, Utah, another garden spot, where we slept in huts covered with tar paper, thus ensuring that the frying 100-degree heat was kept cozily within the enclosures. It was a nomadic period for me, since I was subsequently sent to the state of Washington, near the northern border, where the winter was comparable to lazing the days away in Hudson's Bay. On New Year's Eve I had drawn guard duty and was lurching back and forth in the snow, every fiber alert for invaders from Canada, when I heard, in the distance, some church bells announcing midnight and the New Year. I looked around, and the only other living being in sight was a stray dog, of the sort that always hangs around army bases. I hunkered down in the snow and called him over. He was wet and mangy, in other words a mirror image of myself, and riddled with self-pity. I said, "Happy New Year, doggie," at which precise moment the dog peed on me.

After six months or so, things got better. I was assigned to the Sixth Army Band, at 6th army headquarters in San Francisco. Al-though I was supposed to write a lot of music for the band, any-thing and everything necessary, I had to play a band instrument as well. Well, possibly not really play, but at least be able to hold it convincingly. I opted for flute and piccolo, for the obvious reasons of their minimum weight, and tried to teach myself the rudiments of playing them. My fingers soon knew their way about, at least sufficiently for marches, but my lip and breath weren't geared for wind expertise, and I would turn an alarming shade of vermilion trying to master the descant in "Under the Double Eagle."

Luckily, my lack of flute talent was not a major problem, and I set to writing endless arrangements for brass band, the inevitable marches as well as completely bizarre band transcriptions of Shostakovich's First Symphony and Chabrier's *España*.

San Francisco appealed to me immediately. It is one of the very few American cities with an unmistakable style. I have often felt that the central parts of most cities in the United States are interchangeable; while on long tours, I have awakened and looked out of the hotel window onto the streets of Cleveland, Detroit, Cincinnati, or any of a dozen others, without knowing my precise whereabouts. This is not the case in San Francisco, and I enjoyed myself even though I was flat broke. To be stony bust and still enjoy a city is not possible in too many places.

Jazz was very popular with the college crowd in the fifties, and San Francisco had its share of famous clubs. The Blackhawk and Facks were doing a teeming business, and I managed to nurse one beer long enough to be initiated into the then mysterious new world of Dizzy Gillespie, Charlie Parker, the MJQ, and Bud Powell. What I heard scared me at first, and I stopped playing until I could begin to assimilate these new and remarkable sounds. That particular year, 1952, changed my view of jazz forever, and I began to sit in with the newer crowd on the bandstands of these clubs.

I was helped with my tentative steps toward the new jazz by my army friends. In the band barracks were several battered record players and I began to hear new sounds as purveyed by names new to me. At first I simply thought Charlie Parker's sound was too harsh and aggressive, but it didn't take me long before I heard the beauty behind it, and the limitless invention.

Dizzy Gillespie's playing instantly attracted me, rule-breaking and irresistible. In 1950 a revered name only to a relatively few listeners, Dizzy is now the grand old man, the *eminence grise,* loaded down with honors and awards, but still a huge presence and still as puckish as ever. Dizzy has always had a finely honed way of summing up a situation. At the first Newport Jazz Festival, he was standing on the sidelines, watching the scene with interest. The society audience sat on the lawn in little gilt chairs, like the ones at couturiers' showings. Most everyone was in a white dinner jacket and sported raw silk bow ties and bemused expressions. Onstage, the Count Basie band was roaring through one of their specials, a steaming, cooking force of nature, and the dressed-up local audience was trying to hang on. The owner of the estate and the sponsor of the festival, Mrs. Lorillard, made her way across the lawn and approached Dizzy, yards of tulle surrounding her. She smiled a bright, nervous smile.

"What do you think of all this, Mr. Gillespie?" she asked, a sweeping gesture indicating the acreage. Dizzy nodded at her without a trace of irony.

"I think it's the end of tennis," he said.

But I've digressed. Here I was in the barracks, hunched over a Woolworth's record player, trying to figure out the new superimposed harmonies and the liberated rhythm sections. One of the members of the army band was Chet Baker, then a fledgling but already in full possession of his remarkable and lovely trumpet technique, and not far off from becoming very famous indeed, at least in the insular jazz world. Whenever a pass into town was available, I would go to the Blackhawk, at the corner of Turk and Hyde, and listen with all my might. Chet would go as well, but the difference between us was that he would sit in with whatever group was performing, and was welcomed and admired. Chet was the only musician I know who actually practiced himself out of the Army. After lights out, and during any minute or hour of precious free time, he would retire into the communal toilets and start practicing. For hours on end. Nothing stopped him, nothing dissuaded him. Finally, after futile warnings and punishments, he was adjudged unfit for military life, and demobilized. Chet changed into a better-fitting suit, unpacked his horn, and went back to the clubs to play, except now he was getting paid for it.

Being less inventive in my methods, I had to wait until my official release from the service to apply for work in the jazz clubs. During the days I was studying with Pierre Monteux, trying to unravel the mysteries of Stravinsky, and at night I sat with a rhythm section of my choosing and attempted to update my improvising. My favorite San Francisco club, the Blackhawk, was run by a large and good-natured man named Guido Caccianti. Guido treated the musicians wonderfully well. He would lend them money, feed them if necessary, and he was solicitous of their instruments and their safety. He would stand behind the bar and grin with pleasure at the music emanating from the bandstand. When the music turned to a slow ballad, Guido would reach behind the bar and come up with a dark pink gel, which he would clamp over the spotlight and hold in place with his left hand. It was his own artistic touch, and he took this additional job very seriously. We all appreciated the effort. The bandstand itself was typical. Small, dark, and uncomfortable. There were heavy gray drapes flanking the little platform; they were voluminous and took up quite some space. One day we were rehearsing in the club during the day. A jazz club during the day is not the most aesthetically pleasing environment known to man. Nothing has ever been aired out, and sunshine has not been allowed in since before Miss Havisham was stood up. The nighttime conviviality and coziness are gone, and the scarred tables and dented chrome chairs are not pretty. I noticed that the curtains draping the bandstand were extremely dusty; in fact, to my eye, they seemed made of solidified dust.

"We ought to tell Guido these need cleaning," I said.

My drummer, Gene Gammage, nodded. "Yeah," he said gloomily, "they look beat." Whereupon he hauled off and smacked one of the curtains, in the manner of a carpet being beaten on a clothes line. What we expected was a cloud of dust, but we had been optimistic. The curtains actually broke into pieces. I have never seen this phenomenon since. Great pieces of ancient velveteen broke off and fell on the floor, where they disintegrated.

Guido was philosophical. "They were here when I bought the place," he explained.

As club owners go, he was a favorite of the musicians. There were some pretty rough types elsewhere, and Guido certainly was hipper to the needs of the players than an entrepreneur in Detroit who, after listening to complaints about the musical condition of the piano from Oscar Peterson, George Shearing, and me, finally gave in and had it painted. I didn't really know what Guido's background was, and I didn't care. One night, after closing, I was out on the sidewalk trying to remind my lungs what fresh air was, when an extremely belligerent drunk came over and began to harangue at me. It was the custom of the Blackhawk to pay its artists in cash at the end of a week, and I was, at the time, clutching the paper bag into which my salary had been wadded. I had definite visions of my drunken adversary making a grab at this bag, and probably slugging me with something nasty at the same time. Suddenly the door opened, and Guido wandered over to us. He was in his shirtsleeves and his expression was perfectly calm. He put his fingertips on the front of the drunk's jacket, and without raising his voice above the conversational level, he said "Good night, friend." The drunk fell apart like a dandelion in a strong wind.

"Geez, I'm sorry, Guido," he managed and disappeared down the street. Guido stared after him for a few seconds; then he turned to me. "Don't worry about it," he said, "I'll get you a cab."

I MADE FRIENDS with Norman Carol, another musician stationed at the Presidio. He was even then a most remarkable violinist. Shortly after his discharge from the army he became the concertmaster of the Philadelphia Orchestra, a distinguished position he has now held for thirty-odd years. But back in 1951, neither one of us could have laid claim to the adjective "distinguished" by the wildest stretch of the imagination. Whenever it was possible, we would commandeer a piano and play sonatas for our own pleasure, and I remember quite a few evenings at officers' clubs, trying to make some Viennese bonbons audible above the hubbub.

Norman and I were summoned to appear at the office of the reigning two-star general one day. We absolutely could not figure out why. Our small transgressions of the rules were definitely not worthy of generals, and neither one of us could come up with a reason to receive a medal. So we shined our boots, pressed our wrinkled ties, and polished our belt buckles, hoping that our smart appearance might lessen whatever blow was to be aimed at us. The general was feeling chatty. "I'm told you two can play the fiddle and the piano pretty good," he said. "Well, in two weeks' time there's going to be a huge meeting of heads of state here in Frisco;

Truman is coming, and so are the Russians, the English, the French, and everybody else. After the meetings are over, there's gonna be a big blowout at the Palace Hotel, and I want you to play for a half hour or so. Understood?"

We nodded rapidly. Yes, we understood. We thank the general, sir. We'll do our best, sir, yes indeed. We saluted and backed away from the desk, treading on each other's feet and bumping into a map case. When we got to the door, the general said rather sharply, "Oh, there's one thing I forgot. You mustn't play anything recognizably national. Nothing American or Russian or French or English. Understood?"

We looked at one another. Obviously this request was both loony and impossible to fulfill. My misplaced compulsion for jokes surfaced. "If the general agrees," I said winningly, "we could play a long Swiss medley."

Not a blink, not a smile was forthcoming. "That'll be fine. See to it," and the general turned away from us. Silently we went outside. Once we were in the street, Norman turned on me. "You moron," he started, "you asshole, what are we going to do now? A Swiss medley, you jerk! Name me some Swiss composers except Bloch and Frank Martin! We'll be court-martialed!"

I calmed him down. "Nobody'll be listening, Norman," I said with confidence. "And if by chance anyone does listen, what makes you think they'll recognize the music?" As it turned out, I was right. The ballroom of the Palace Hotel was alive with bunting and flags, the guests were representatives of the world's power, and they were not interested in the two GIs on a small corner platform, assaying Brahms, Debussy, and Prokofiev. We ate a lot of very good food, drank a glass or two of wine, and ogled the great and powerful. Our general passed, retinue in tow. This was one night when he was outranked, but he was very scary to us. He gave us the briefest of glances and smiled a smile which never reached his eyes.

"Well done, boys," he said. "Carry on."

DURING THE YEAR I was able to spend in San Francisco, I made one contact that changed my life. I met Pierre Monteux, one of the most renowned conductors of the twentieth century. He was, at that time, the music director of the San Francisco Symphony, and a teacher of near-legendary reputation. My introduction to him was effected by Leonard Bernstein, who had come through town on a tour with the Israel Philharmonic. Typically enough, he said, "I just don't understand why you don't know Pierre," as if it were somehow fraudulent to be a musician without being in Monteux's circle of friends or pupils. I was so in awe of Le Maître that I could hardly speak upon first meeting him. My mind kept going back to the fact that here was the conductor of the premiere of Stravinsky's *Rite of Spring,* an evening that had changed the face of music history, and it was difficult for me to identify this small, bustling, rotund and cheerful man as such a giant. Thank goodness Monteux took a liking to me; he did not hold my commercial work against me in the least, but he did instill in me an enormous desire to learn and to better myself. We made an agreement: During the time I was stationed in San Francisco, he would see me whenever it was mutually possible, and I agreed, almost overcome with gratitude, to stay on in the city once I had been returned to civilian life, and to postpone my return to Hollywood.

His knowledge was incredible; it seemed to me there was absolutely nothing pertaining to music that he didn't know. His methods were sometimes eccentric. He passed me on the street once and, as a greeting, asked me, "What's the lowest possible trill on an oboe, ah, too late, too late!" and went toddling off without a backward glance. Even if I had known the answer, I wouldn't have had the presence of mind to answer him in a split second; as it was, I didn't know the answer but boy! did I ever look it up! Monteux was almost completely unaware of the more worldly happenings around him. I don't believe he ever took in the fact that I was in uniform; I think he was under the impression that I liked ill-fitting brown clothes. This was emphasized one day when I told him, after my lesson ended, that I very probably would be put on the next set of overseas orders to be sent to Japan. Maître received this information quite seriously, frowned, then spoke in his almost music-hall French accent.

"Listen, my dear," he said, "you are making a mistake. Oh, I know that the orchestra in Tokyo is meant to be good, but believe me, I have heard them, and the winds and brass are very undernourished. Strings are all right, but you can do as well without traveling such a distance."

What he taught me, that year and after, is impossible to describe. Technically he was a walking textbook. As a human being he had strength and grace, and he imparted knowledge without impatience. He liked cloaking his advice with indirection and irony. A few years later he saw me conduct a concert with a provincial orchestra. He came backstage after the performance. He paid me some compliments and then asked, "In the last movement of the Haydn Symphony, my dear, did you think the orchestra was playing well?" My mind whipped through the movement; had there been a mishap, had something gone wrong? Finally, and fearing the worst, I said that yes, I thought the orchestra had indeed played very well. Monteux leaned toward me conspiratorially and smiled. "So did I," he said. "Next time, don't interfere!" It was advice to be followed forever, germinal and important. I've conducted literally thousands of concerts in the decades following my studies with him, but I've never forgotten anything he said to me.

The final months of my two-year army tenure were spent at Camp Stoneman, California, waiting for my discharge. The last four weeks seemed like a year. Finally, the appointed day dawned. I was given a large piece of paper, with designated places for twenty officers to sign me out—at the motor pool, at the supply depot, by the weapons officer, by the barracks cadre, by everyone imaginable. The last signature was finally affixed and I stood at the camp gate and showed the document to the sergeant of the guard. "Okay, Sarge," he said—I had made sergeant by that time—"you're through, you can leave." I wanted to make absolutely, definitely, unchangeably sure. "There's nothing else, nothing?" I inquired. "Nope," answered this wonderful man, "you can consider yourself a civilian." I stepped away from the guard hut and onto the highway, which had visible heat waves rising from the macadam. Carefully I opened my duffel bag, took out the civilian clothes I had bought in advance of the great event, and proceeded to strip off my uniform right on the glaring street. I put on the new clothes and made a bundle of my army gear, tying it up neatly with the sleeves. There was a gigantic refuse can about fifty yards down the road, and I walked over and dropped the past two years into it. Then I caught the bus into San Francisco, and before I checked into a hotel near The Black Hawk, I bought myself a pink shirt.

I SUPPOSE jazz musicians have always been privy to the occasional veiled sentence uttered by owners whose lifestyle was patterned after the less savory cast members of Humphrey Bogart movies. A few years later, I was working in Las Vegas with a good trio, Red Mitchell and Don Lamond. We were making a good deal of money, but we were by no stretch of the imagination a hit. What we played was not to the liking of the customers, and what the customers wanted was not to our liking. After a few days of unnerving failure, I went to see the boss of the casino. He wore pinkie rings and sprayed his hair with attar of roses. I explained to him that I was aware that we were not making his guests happy with our brand of music, and I that I thought we were therefore taking his money under false pretenses. Why don't we quit, I suggested; it had been a mistake all around, I would be happy to let him out of the contract, he could get a group better suited to his room, and we would go off to more receptive fields ourselves. "Well, that's very nice of you," he said. "Very classy. But lemme explain something to you. We like having entertainers and musicians in my casino who have a name value. It looks good on the marquee outside. You made some good records and you had some publicity just now when you came out of the army. Frankly, I don't give a crap whether the customers like the music or not, I think you oughta stay for the rest of your contract."

I was oblivious of the danger signals. "But Milton," I said, voice ringing with sincerity, "this is silly. I'm wasting your money and you're wasting my time. I think I should hand in my notice."

"Maybe you weren't listening," said Milton. "I want you to stay. I want you to reconsider. I think it would be smart." He leaned back and his pinkie ring glistened under the lamp.

I almost laughed. What was this, a scene from a thirties movie? Was I talking to Sydney Greenstreet? "Let me understand something," I said. "You're not actually threatening me, are you?"

Milton's smile was prompt. "Threatening you? Don't be silly, I'm not threatening you. That's not my department."

Not my department? All my nerve ends suddenly came to life.

Whose department was it? Evidently the "department" existed. I mumbled something about thinking it over, left his office, and went out into the club. Gower Champion was sitting at the bar. He was still doing a dance act with his wife Marge, and they were a smash at another hotel down the road. Gower was an old hand at Vegas experiences. I relayed my conversation to him and asked his advice. He gave it with alacrity. "Are you kidding?" he demanded. "Are you really that naive? Is this worth being beaten up in the parking lot?"

I was incredulous. This was 1952! This couldn't happen! Luckily, I was not only amazed but also cowardly, I knocked on Milton's door and stuck my head in. "I've been thinking," I said, "and I guess we'll stay for the rest of the three weeks." Milton was reading some papers at his desk. He did not bother to look up. "Good," he said. "Thank you."

During the late fifties and sixties I was active in jazz circles. I performed a lot, met many of the protagonists, and made a lot of friends. Only very recently did I get back to that pursuit (even though it is only sporadic) and I found that jazz musicians, possibly more than their classical counterparts, wear long-standing friendships easily and gracefully. Their friendships are not influenced by advancement through social contact, and tend to be governed by a very simple rule: If they like the way you play, and if they believe you to be a nice fellow, then fine. If one of those two elements is badly missing, forget it.

The lifestyle of these musicians is nomadic, to put it mildly. Endless changes of venue are the norm, and it is not at all rare to lose touch with a friend for a period of a year or more. (Recently, while I was sitting in the offices of Ronald Wilford, the head of Columbia Artists and the man who started me on my career as a conductor, we were planning my concert calendar for a few seasons hence. I looked at the proposed schedule and said, "I think I'm spending too much time on the road." Ronald winced, and said gently, "We prefer calling it 'touring.'") I have never heard of a jazz musician complaining, "You never even called me once," or "Where have you been?"

It's not for lack of caring or that they aren't glad to see you, but chances are they haven't been that easy to find either, so why be accusatory? Only six months ago I went back into a recording studio to make the first jazz album I had made in twenty-five years, and I had taken out fail-safe insurance in the presence of Ray Brown, the indefatigable and brilliant bassist, and Joe Pass, a guitarist whose technique and inventiveness leave his colleagues open-mouthed. I knew them both well, I had worked with both of them a generation earlier, and we had been friends at that time. I walked into the studio, a quarter century of classical concerts later, and was instantly received with the kind of relaxed warmth usually based on twice-weekly dinners. Lots of jokes, some reminiscing, some future planning, and a great deal of music making. I can't remember an easier record to make, and I went home in the early hours of the morning with my nerves quiescent, my blood pressure down, and in a generally euphoric fog.

Ray Brown, in a sudden spurt of philosophical musing, said, "Being a jazz musician is a very unnatural and tough way to make a living. Too many of the guys die very early, much too young. The way I figure it, if you can lead a jazz musician's life and make it past thirty-five, chances are good you'll be around at ninety."

Quite a number of illustrious players opted for a life less given to excessive strain and turned to the film studios for work. Shelly Manne, Shorty Rogers, Lennie Niehaus, Bob Cooper, Russ Freeman, Mundell Lowe, Neal Hefti, and Johnny Mandel all were successful and active, trading in a part of their previous existence for soft shirts, California sunshine, and station wagons in the San Fernando Valley. They added a lot to the recording stage atmosphere; not only their obvious brilliance as players, but also a sort of laconic, wry understanding of the egos they saw bouncing off the walls.

The 1990 teenagers feel that they have coined both the term "cool" and the mannerisms that illustrate the word, but they are in fact a good thirty-five years too late to claim that invention. Jazz players have always been unfazed by outbursts of temper, threats and bribes, or even the sight of a good friend walking in with a totally unexpected new lady. Therefore, they were a wonderful influence in the Hollywood recording studios. Judy Garland, in one of her fabled temper explosions, was causing producers and directors to cower, ashen-faced, in the corner. She suddenly wheeled around and saw Larry Bunker, a wonderful drummer, standing within the periphery of her vision. "And what the hell do you think you're looking at?" she screamed. Larry looked at her with admiration. "Gee," he said calmly, "just like in the movies!" Judy, who was basically funny and self-deprecating, started laughing.

I was bailed out once as well. During a technically very complicated recording at Goldwyn Studios, one of the playback machines broke down time and time again, causing endless delays. Finally I succumbed to the luxury of pointless anger. "How long do we all have to sit here waiting?" I shouted loudly. "Why can't this thing be fixed, and fixed *now?*" I finished this Wagnerian moment and turned rather imperiously. Right next to me, seated at the orchestral piano, was the great jazz pianist Russ Freeman, a good friend. He leaned over so he could whisper to me. "Can I stay and watch you wig out, man?" he asked, a man interested in the answer. I was very grateful. One small put-down, friend to friend, had saved me from acting like a total ass.

My closest friend among the jazz players was the incomparable drummer Shelly Manne. He could play anything, in any style, and enjoyed almost all of it. He was a superb musician. I have always held the theory that percussionists fall into two categories: the ones who are deeply involved in music, schooled in most of its intricacies, and sensitive to everything being played around them; and then there are the others who just hit whatever drum is in front of them. Shelly was almost definitely of the former school. Bartok could move him to tears, and so could Ellington.

He was also fearless, and his boundless good nature allowed him to get away with actions that would have resulted in lesser musicians being called out behind the Louvre at dawn. Once I was visiting a recording of *West Side Story* with a gigantic orchestra, dancers, and singers cluttering up every inch of spare space. In charge of the musicians was Johnny Green, who for some reason took out his nervousness by picking on Shelly. Shelly remained cool and impervious, but then the slanging became more serious and climaxed with Johnny on the podium—Caesar reviewing the troops—demanding, "Well, don't you have anything at all to say, Shelly?"

Shelly stood up and came forward through the orchestra. Everyone fell apprehensively silent. Johnny stood waiting, veins throbbing. He was wearing a pure white linen turtleneck buttoned up to his chin, the very picture of conductorial splendor. Shelly stood in front of the podium, tilted his head up, and opened his mouth very wide. "Doctor, could you look at this tooth, please? It's been throbbing all night." Johnny was defeated, the orchestra laughed with relief, and work continued.

Sometime within the past two years, an employee of the management of the Los Angeles Philharmonic voiced a few complaints about me to members of that orchestra. The gentleman was disappointed by the fact that I wasn't commanding enough at rehearsals and that the atmosphere was often lighthearted. Tom Stevens, the principal trumpet, explained it. "André never got over being a player himself," he said approvingly. His answer was misunderstood totally and the instant response was, "Exactly, that's the whole problem!"

Tom related this story to me with noneditorializing amusement. I was happy to hear his compliment. I hope I never get over being a player.

FOUR

JAZZ AND THE ARMY were only an interlude. Soon I was back at MGM, where the studio had a new boss. Mayer's successor was a tall, affable, likable man named Dore Schary. He had put in some years as a screenwriter and had produced some successful films at RKO before becoming Mayer's second in command. It wasn't long before new names were painted on the office doors and Dore became the Master of All He Surveyed. From time to time he would personally produce a film at MGM (as opposed to impersonally supervising the rest of the product), and I was tapped to compose the music for two of these efforts. The first one was actually a hell of a good movie, *Bad Day at Black Rock*, with a superb performance by Spencer Tracy. It dealt quite realistically with prejudice during the Second World War years, and Schary had a specific wish for the music.

"I want it to sound military," he said. "Lots of French horns," and to emphasize his wish, his arms pumped out the unmistakable gestures of a slide trombone.

"You mean," I began carefully, "that you want a lot of brass instruments?"

"No no no"—a little impatiently—"French horns, lots of them," and again the charade of a very busy trombonist.

"Fine, okay," I agreed, and proceeded to write a vaguely dissonant and sinister score that seemed to make the producer very happy.

My other assignment started out disastrously, and it was entirely due to my stupidity. Schary had produced a film called *Designing Woman,* with Lauren Bacall and Gregory Peck. The picture was finished and edited and I was invited to see it, along with quite a few others. Now, the run-of-the-mill producers had these screenings in one of the studio projection rooms, but Dore had the clout to run them in his own living room. He was a hospitable man and invited about ten of us to dinner prior to the running of the film. His house was furnished in Early Unamerican, with every room crammed and stuffed with spinning wheels, weather vanes, quilts, salt boxes and whirligigs, and primitive portraits, most of them made in Taiwan. The dinner was enormous and the wine was heavy. After a sickeningly rich dessert, I made my torpid way into the living room. I sat in a very soft chair. The lights were dimmed at the flick of a switch, the prize Grant Wood slid soundlessly upward, disclosing a screen, the film started, and I went into a deep, dreamless, happy, babylike sleep. I woke for the first time when the lights went back on, and realized that I had not seen a single frame of the movie. I had not been given a script to read and I didn't know whether *Designing Woman* was a biography of some designer, or of Mata Hari, or of the only female member of the Bauhaus. Mr. Schary smiled at me.

"Well, André, do you have unusual ideas of what you'd like to compose for this?" I went into a sort of manic overdrive. I couldn't very well admit that I hadn't seen a single frame of his brainchild because I had had the best sleep in months, and so I improvised rashly.

"Dore," I said with conviction, "I'd like to write the whole score for just strings and harp, and possibly piano."

Dore was stumped, but game. "Just strings, eh kid?" he said. "I would never have thought of that, but listen, what the hell, by all means try it."

The next morning I was at the studio bright and early and looked up Benny Lewis, the film editor of *Designing Woman.* I wasted no time. "Benny, can you run me the film again, right away, please?"

"I can't get a projection room this morning, André, and aren't you a bit anxious?" he asked. I confessed the whole predicament and he laughed until the tears ran down his face. "Come into the cutting room," he offered, then ran the whole film for me on a

Moviola, which is a great clattering machine used by film editors and has a viewing screen of approximately four inches. Two hours later I realized that "just strings and a harp" had been total nonsense, but now I was stuck with it, and actually the challenge was advantageous. I wrote a light and pleasant comedy score, it all fitted quite reasonably, and everyone was happy. I had been lucky, but it was a near thing.

BUSBY BERKELEY has been the object of more veneration and admiration than any other director of musicals from the thirties and forties. His kaleidoscopic views of girls, the flowering of humans making intricate patterns, and the gorgeously staged excesses of giant pianos, shimmering legs, fluorescent violins, and geometric patterns of dancers have been analyzed almost out of existence by scholars of the cinema, and there are serious film students who can list every shot in the "Shadow Waltz" number with the earnestness of an archaeologist poring over recently found Roman shards. I had admired and been vastly amused by his later work as well, by the endless mobility of the conga number for Judy Garland and Mickey Rooney, and by the hilariously phallic "Banana" ballet for Carmen Miranda.

He was a man who venerated the camera and adored setting problems for it, then coming up with solutions. He was patient with all the machinery he set into complicated motion, and he deeply appreciated the artisans who made his visions possible. At the same time, he was utterly without sympathy or compassion for the actors who flinched with fear as his giant cranes swooped and roared around the set. He would sit behind the careening camera, his eyes blazing, shouting directions and exhortations while the playback music added to the atmosphere of panic.

"Great, great," he would scream, "the green smoke is perfect, let's have more, yes, that's lovely, now, whip the mirrors around, wonderful, just right, get those prisms ready for the waterfall, oh boy that's perfect," and suddenly the head swerved and the voice screamed in anguish, "Goddammit, you silly bitch, can't you dance any faster?"

But more recently he had been quiescent, and so I was excited to hear that he had been hired to stage the numbers in a film called

Small Town Girl, which starred Jane Powell and Farley Granger. The script was an impenetrable mess and I had dreaded working on it, but suddenly I was looking forward to meeting, and actually working with, the legendary Berkeley. He sat behind his desk, shuffling storyboard cards—individual drawings of each proposed camera setup—and he looked up briefly to wave me closer. He was not an imposing figure, and the features of his face didn't really match, like a toy that has been mended hastily.

"Look at this," he began without preamble, "I'd like Janie Powell to make an entrance in a small buggy drawn by forty eagles. Do you think Joe Pasternak will okay that? It's likely to be pretty expensive."

It was difficult, but I managed to stay impassive. He paused and smiled very faintly. "By God, you didn't even flinch," he said. Well, the producer did flinch, quite severely, and the forty eagles had to be filed away for future use.

In no way daunted, Buzz (no one called him Busby) decided that the buggy could also be drawn quite picturesquely by a huge ox. One ox, although an unusual request, was a lot cheaper than forty eagles, so the animal was duly procured, hitched up to a dainty buggy, and shown to the director. Buzz walked around him critically.

"He's okay," he said, "nice and big, but I want him painted gold." The extraordinary thing was that no one on the set questioned this even for a moment. The various assistant directors set up the cry "Paint the ox gold!" and it echoed around the huge set. At this point lunch was called. Early in the afternoon Buzz went inspecting again. There stood the ox, gleaming in gold paint, with a large red plush heart hung around his neck for good measure. He looked deeply silly, and the animal was obviously very embarrassed. Berkeley made a camera frame of his hands and peered as he walked closer. "I can see that you only sprayed color on the top part, underneath he doesn't look at all gold," and he knelt down and gave close scrutiny to the ox's nether regions.

I won't quibble about the fact that my repertoire of unusual animal experiences was perhaps too small to cope with what happened next. The ox had had it, in spades—enough was enough. He took careful aim and peed right on Mr. Berkeley, who was still on his knees underneath. The fact that Buzz was wearing a white suit was a nice touch, but the force, trajectory, and amount of the stream overshadowed everything else; it was awe-inspiring, a fire engine of bovine revenge. As Buzz was rescued, bundled up in huge towels, and led away to a dressing room, I couldn't help admiring the ox and wondering what the forty eagles would have done to assert their dignity.

It was in the staging of a number for Ann Miller that Buzz really came into his own on that film. *Small Town Girl* was relentlessly wholesome, with the characters behaving in a way that made Andy Hardy resemble the Marquis de Sade. Therefore, when Berkeley was given carte blanche to stage a song called "I Gotta Hear That Beat," he instantly transcended its banality and went into a manic high gear. He devised a dance in which Ann Miller, tapping madly, cruised around a huge floor that had dozens of holes in it. As she passed these holes, arms holding instruments would pop out, arms in tuxedo sleeves, brandishing trumpets, trombones, clarinets, string instruments, and drumsticks. These disembodied hands actually belonged to dancers or extras who were lying on their backs under the floor, unseen and unsung, waiting for their cues in order to whip their arms out at precisely the moment the lyrics dictated. It must have been over 100 degrees under the floor, and completely dark, and the hapless extras had to be hauled out periodically for air and light. They would stand, white-faced and drenched, gulping air for a few precious minutes before being wedged back under the floor again. There were musical problems as well; whatever instruments came out of the holes had to be heard on the soundtrack at the same time, and it was almost impossible to time the traveling dance steps to the precise fraction of seconds necessary. As usual, Buzz was endlessly patient and solicitous of all the technical people, the light movers, the camera pullers, the track layers, and almost completely incognizant of the human travail required. It was a scene worthy of Fritz Lang's *Metropolis:* There was Ann Miller, spangled and glittering, whirling around dangerously, avoiding the holes in the floor; there were the subterranean instrument holders, gasping for air; and above it all, Buzz, on the seat of a huge camera crane, shouting imprecations, screaming instructions, hurling the camera around at an alarming speed, Ben Hur during the chariot race, Errol Flynn leading the Charge of the Light Brigade, General Custer heading right into the Indians at full gallop.

AN EVEN GREATER GOOD FORTUNE was to work with "The Freed Unit" —the most prestigious, self-contained group of people on the Culver City lot. The list of musicals Arthur Freed had produced was amazing. Starting with the Judy Garland–Mickey Rooney films and carrying on through *Cabin in the Sky, Meet Me in St. Louis, An American in Paris, Singin' in the Rain, Gigi, Ziegfeld Follies, Easter Parade, The Harvey Girls, Show Boat, Annie Get your Gun, The Band Wagon*—an impressive achievement. He brought Vincente Minnelli to Hollywood, as well as Betty Comden and Adolph Green, Lerner and Loewe, Oliver Smith, Cole Porter, Cecil Beaton, and a parade of others. He was not very social, and quite taciturn, and sometimes he seemed a far cry from the dynamo his reputation had painted him. A few nights before the filming of *Gigi* began, a group of us were having dinner in Paris, at the Mediterranée Restaurant— Cecil Beaton, Vincente Minnelli, Alan Jay Lerner, Fritz Loewe, myself, Joe Ruttenberg, Preston Ames, Hermione Gingold, and Louis Jourdan. Hermione said that she had been wondering about something. "I know Mr. Freed's credits," she said, "and they're phenomenal. You've all worked with him before, but it's my first time. I keep watching him, but he doesn't seem to be doing much. What is it that he does that's so special?"

Alan gave her the answer. "Well," he said, looking around the table, "we're all here, aren't we?"

During my years in Culver City, Arthur Freed was the most complex and interesting producer I worked for. He adored talent, and he went out of his way to help and promote creative people. He also knew quite a bit about French painting, and he took immense pleasure in raising orchids. At the same time, he was tough and occasionally ruthless, but if you had done good work for him, he was forever loyal and would hire you time and time again.

He had certain foibles, however, which took some getting used to. He simply could not admit to not having seen something, not having heard something, not having been someplace. This sometimes reached wonderfully zany proportions. One night at Ira Gershwin's, Arthur wandered into the room where Ira, Gene Kelly,

Michael Kidd, and I were watching the live television coverage of that night's basketball game. "What're you looking at, fellas?" he inquired.

"The Lakers game," said Gene. Arthur didn't miss a beat.

"Oh yeah," he muttered, "I saw it yesterday."

There were certain problems Arthur had no fondness for. He was used to dealing with the big stuff—buying that year's Broadway smash, hiring Cole Porter, devising huge budgets for his next project—but the day-to-day problems during the shooting of a film were anathema. One day I went up to his office and asked to see him. I found him behind his desk, looking at a book of Braque reproductions. "Arthur," I began, "there's a problem. Gene wants to record his big number next Monday, but in order to do that we have to postpone the ballad for Cyd. Which would you like me to prepare?"

Arthur sat, posing for Rodin. Suddenly he stood up. "Just one minute, okay, André?" he said, and left the room. I figured he went to the bathroom, always a good place for decisions, and I waited. And waited. And waited. I looked at the Braque book. Finally I ventured into the outer office and asked, "Helen, where's Mr. Freed?" Helen was her unflappable self and gave me a charming smile. "Mr. Freed went home," she told me. The message was clear; I answered my own question, prepared one of the numbers (I don't remember which one), and production went ahead quite calmly.

In Paris, when we were making *Gigi*, Arthur expressed a desire to see the treasures of Notre Dame and asked me to see whether it would be possible. His French was not up to it. I agreed with alacrity; the prospect was lovely. An old priest met us and escorted us down the nave to the chancel and behind a screen. A reliquary of the head of Charlemagne was brought out, along with other examples of ecclesiastical splendor.

I was entranced, as was Arthur. He asked some knowledgeable and pertinent questions, which I translated, and the priest was happy to be the guide to so much beauty. And then Arthur suddenly forgot where he was, reached into his pocket, shook a cigarette out of a pack, snapped his gold lighter, and blew a luxurious cloud of smoke into the chapel. Our host, after a moment's paralysis, went a little mad. A flood of French enveloped us, and I started tugging at Arthur, stage-whispering and hissing at him. "What's the matter with you two?" Arthur demanded, peering through the smoke. "The cigarette, Arthur, the cigarette, put it out, get rid of it, are you mad?" He looked mildly surprised. "Okay, sorry," he said, dropping the offending object on the floor in front of the altar and stepping on it. Our exit from Notre Dame is, mercifully, a bit hazy in my memory. I do know that my French vocabulary reached new heights of prolixity and that I importuned any and all available saints not to take offense. Arthur, of course, remained oblivious and a bit absentminded through it all.

For a man so susceptible to beauty, he had weird reactions. One night, again in Paris, I succumbed to one of the world's great tourist attractions and took the *bateau-mouche,* the boat that sails up and down the Seine for a few evening hours. I stood at the railing, floored by the views. The air was soft and purplish, and the reflections of the bridges shimmered in the water like so many Monets. It was all the picture postcards rolled into one, but it was real and achingly beautiful. The next morning, on the set, I told Arthur about it. At first he was hesitant, should he really go? Would he really enjoy it? I told him how wonderful it had seemed to me. Two days later he wandered over to me. "I went on that boat you told me about," he said. "I didn't think much of it. The food was lousy."

Never mind. It was a pleasure to work on his films, and some of the most talented and fascinating people in the performing arts left their mark on his musicals. He did me many favors. Once, when I was assigned to a particularly boring film, he found out about it and insisted I be put to work on the preparation of an entirely fictitious future musical for him instead. He yelled bloody murder at me when I did a hurried and rather slipshod recording for him, called me names and generally turned apoplectic, but he took it as a matter of course that I would again be his music director on the next film.

I'm almost glad he isn't around anymore, now that musical films have degenerated into the screeching and wailing of the adolescent pop stars of the week, leering with teenage concupiscence and flashing their pimples. He wouldn't have known what to make of them. Come to think of it, none of us do.

One of the eight films I did for Freed was *It's Always Fair Weather,* in 1954. Gene Kelly, Dan Dailey, and Michael Kidd were the three dancing stars, Gene and Stanley Donen directed, Betty Comden and Adolph Green wrote the script and the lyrics, and I composed the music and conducted. When the film was finished, MGM decided to go all-out and have a press showing at the studio, in the subterranean projection room, which had ultracomfortable chairs and gave the impression of a first-class lounge on a second-class ocean liner. Everyone was invited, the cream of the journalists: *Life, Time, Newsweek, Look,* the *New York Times, The Saturday Evening Post,* the lot. Canapes and champagne were served at seven o'clock, the film to be shown at eight. By seven-thirty the crowd was considerable and I escaped upstairs and out onto the steps of the Thalberg Building to get a breath of air and watch the purple California dusk for a while. A taxi drew up to the front of the building. A tall lady in a white dress got out, paid, and began to make her way—rather unsteadily—up the steps to where I was standing. She wore white "shorty" gloves and her ensemble was topped off by a large green hat, of the sort worn at garden parties. As the lady came nearer, I took a closer look, and the worn phrase "my blood ran cold" seems apt. The woman in white was Dan Dailey, happy and sanguine, and drunk.

"Hi," he said, "going down to the screening, are we?"

I tried to put my brain into some kind of gear. If Dan made an entrance downstairs in his white dress, his career would be in smithereens, the new film could be cut up into thousands of little guitar picks, and the studio might be sold as a parking lot. I liked Dan a lot, and admired him as an actor and as a dancer. I had heard vague rumors as to his odd predilection, which evidently had absolutely no basis in homosexuality. When a film assignment was finished, he could afford to relax and perhaps drink a bit too much, and he was given to putting on smart little frocks. It was a sort of hobby, like stamp collecting, or an occasional pursuit like a game of squash. But to get back to the moment at hand, I managed a smile and thought of an emergency plan.

"I was just waiting for you, Dan. I've been asked to intercept you and put you into an office upstairs, so that a couple of newspapermen can get a private interview with you away from the mob, okay?"

I was probably babbling by this time, but Dan was perfectly acquiescent. I wove up the stairs with him and put him into the nearest office, promising to be right back. I then beat every known Olympic record getting back down to the projection room. I looked around and saw Bill Golden, the head of the publicity department, in conversation with the movie critic from *Life* magazine.

"Bill, can I see you for a minute, please?"

Bill looked incredulous. "Not now, all right?" he said out of the side of his mouth.

I had to try again. "Bill, I've really got to talk to you for a minute —*now!*"

Poor Bill. He made vague apologetic hand motions to the critic, turned to me, and hissed, "This better be important, André!"

His admonition did me in. I started to laugh and could not stop. I was hooting and gasping as we made our way across the crowded room. Finally I managed a sentence.

"Well, I've got Dan Dailey waiting upstairs in an office, and he's wearing a white dress and high heels and a green hat, do you think that's important enough?"

Bill's mouth went slack. "Sweet Holy Jesus," he said reverently, then he exited in the manner beloved by Tom and Jerry, where all that is visible is a blur and a puff of smoke. Well, the rest is anticlimactic. Bill and his assistants found Dan, stuffed him into a cold shower, force-fed him black coffee, and got a suit out of the wardrobe department. By the time the film had ended, Dan appeared, dapper and friendly, if a bit subdued, and apologized for being late. None of us ever mentioned the incident again.

I MET Betty Comden and Adolph Green very early in my MGM days. They had come to Hollywood fresh from their Broadway triumphs in order to write the screenplays for *Good News* and their own *On the Town*. They were known then as "the kids" (which they were) and they are still known as "the kids" (which none of us are). They have worked together for so long that it is a popular misconception that they are married. They are not, and come to think of it, neither were Gilbert and Sullivan. Betty and Adolph are more than just attuned to one another, they are sometimes like one person. Nevertheless, they differ wildly from one another. Betty is calm, soft-spoken, and beautiful. Adolph is hyperactive, a born clown, and looks as if he has been exploded onto the earth. His knowledge of music is encyclopedic. He can identify absolutely any fragment of a theme, no matter how arcane or how tunelessly demonstrated, seems to own every classical record ever made, and hasn't missed an interesting concert in decades. If he had turned his roaring energy to being a conductor instead of a writer-lyricist, he would have made all of us look silly. Both Betty and Adolph have a great sense of humor, and their sense of humor ricochets off all four walls. The fact that they are also loyal and sweet friends doesn't hurt.

We had been friends for quite a few years when Arthur Freed assigned us to write the songs for *It's Always Fair Weather*. Betty and Adolph wrote the script and the lyrics; I did the tunes and all the other music for the film. When the first half-dozen numbers had been written, we were asked to play them to Mr. Mayer, no less, and we wended our way to the hallowed snow landscape he called his office. I played the piano and Betty and Adolph told the story, acted out the situations, and performed the songs with the utmost expertise and good nature. Finally our audition was over. There was a pause during which I could have hummed a complete Mahler symphony, and then the oracle spoke.

"Whatever happened to the songs of yesteryear?" he asked musingly. Adolph reacted instantaneously and sprang into action.

"I don't know, I don't know," he shouted, leaping to his feet, "where did I put them? Betty, André, where did we put those songs of yesteryear, can you remember?" and he ran over to a desk in the corner of the office and started shuffling papers and opening drawers. "Didn't we put them somewhere here?"

Betty murmured something about "Oh God, Adolph, one step too far," and we managed to back out of the place, leaving Mr. Mayer behind, fortunately much more bewildered than angry. What saved us, of course, was the fact that our producer, Arthur Freed, had total control over his film unit, and managed to placate L.B., probably telling him that an occasional leave of absence was often granted to the artistic inmates of Bedlam.

. . . .

THERE WAS one other memorable occasion having to do with our playing the songs to someone. We had written a ballad called "Love Is Nothin' but a Racket," and in our euphoria, we thought it was the answer to any prayer Sinatra might have. Ultimately it became sadly evident that *no one,* not Sinatra and not the Three Stooges, would ever do the tune, but we didn't know that at the time. At any rate, off we went, to a building known as the Leading Men's Dressing Rooms, which were permanent rooms (by comparison) for the biggest male stars on the lot. Our plan was to reach Frank during his lunch hour (he was shooting *High Society* at the time) and overwhelm him with a rendition of said number. What we had not reckoned with was the fact that in the film world hierarchy, when stars get to a fairly exalted level, they don't have their names on their doors, so we wandered through a maze of corridors on two floors, knocking gently and opening gingerly, all to no avail. The time allotted to a lunch hour evaporated and we hadn't even found the correct dressing room, much less played the tune. Finally, we were down to the only door we hadn't tried. "This has got to be Frank's," said Betty in a hopeful voice, and we opened the door with some bravado. What greeted our eyes was Sidney Blackmer, a fine character actor who made a great splash in the Broadway version of *Come Back, Little Sheba,* seated in front of his mirror, applying restorative touches of makeup. He looked at our reflection: "Yes?" Sidney had never seen any of us before in his life.

Being around Adolph had rubbed off on me. I turned to him and Betty and said, "Let's do the number for Mr. Blackmer instead!" I crossed the room to the piano, which seemed to be there waiting for us. My two partners didn't blink an eye at the thought but swung right into action. They began to demonstrate, singing and dancing and generally "selling" the tune, while poor Sidney Blackmer, Kleenex tucked into the collar of his shirt to keep it clean from makeup, stood open-mouthed and probably horrorstruck, debating whom to call for help.

Obviously we misbehaved, obviously it was ill mannered and silly, obviously it was arrogant. But what it proves, along with a great many of the other incidents I've recalled, is that we had a good time. We worked hard, but we laughed a great deal, and we enjoyed ourselves. I'm not so sure that is the case in the studios today.

VINCENTE MINNELLI was certainly one of the very best directors of musical films ever. His visual sense was immaculate and his taste impeccable. He was a pleasure to work with and should have given lessons in how to make a film look beautiful and move gracefully. However, Vincente was also given to being nervous and a bit irritable when things did not go smoothly.

An interesting manifestation of this foible came to light on the set of *Kismet,* a turkey if there ever was one, which was being shot in Hollywood in 1955. Vincente was shooting the "Stranger in Paradise" number, during which the young Caliph, serenading his lady love, wanders down a path in the palace gardens. The paths were multicolored gravel, the bushes were laden with exotic blooms, and peacocks strolled through the shot. Now Vincente had an idea. Vic Damone, who played the caliph—could you possibly think of anyone else to play him?—had a very effective high note in the middle of the song, on the words ". . . like a dream, I hang suspended." On the second syllable of the word "suspended," I had thoughtfully provided a shimmering chord in the orchestra, and at this point Vincente wished one of the peacocks to unfurl its gorgeous tail right on cue, a sudden and gigantic fan of colors. The peacock trainer—oh yes, we had a peacock trainer—was called over and given the problem.

His solution was pretty simple: He would lie down behind a prop bush, safely out of camera range, holding a stick with a point on the end of it, much like the implement park cleaners use to spear debris off the grass. On the cue word "suspended," he would jab the stick smartly into the bird's behind, the bird would be surprised and shocked, and *voilà!* a gorgeous fan would be produced. And by God, it worked. Evidently peacocks unfurl all that glory either when courting or when angry, and it certainly could be said that this particular peacock was furious at the indignity.

However, no one had counted on Vincente's famous perfectionism. Two takes, three takes, four takes, still it wasn't good enough. And then the bird got wise. Why stand still and have someone jam a sharp stick up your rear? Maybe this peacock wasn't Stephen

Hawking, but he did figure that one out. And so he would simply move out of reach, scampering away just at the moment when it was necessary for him to provide a stationary target. Half a dozen futile attempts later, Vincente's nerves got the better of him.

"Make him stand still," he yelled at the trainer. "Do something!!"

"Can't do it, Mr. Minnelli," the man apologized. "He's got wise to the trick now."

Vincente was deep in thought. He wasn't about to be beaten by a peacock, not even a smart one. "Prop man," he shouted, and the man came running. "George, see that peacock?" Vincente demanded and George nodded. "Nail him down," said Vincente. "I don't want him to move, nail him down."

It was an interesting moment. George pondered for quite a while. "I can't do that, Mr. Minnelli," he finally offered. "I can't and I won't." Vincente was really jumpy now, a whole set-load of people were waiting, including a small army of "Arabian Nights" extras.

"I tell you, nail him down!" he repeated doggedly. "Or at least do *something,* think of something, and quickly!"

George was an inventive prop man, he liked his work, and he was a good fellow. He invented a sort of bracket, a kind of staple, and duly fastened the bird to the gravel path without actually nailing him. He eyed his invention judiciously and said, "That oughta work," and Vincente screamed for the shot to be lined up again. The playback record was turned on, the orchestra played, Vic Damone hit his high note, the trainer speared the peacock's bum, the peacock flared his tail with abandon, and Vincente was very happy. Next time *Kismet* is on the late show, you might wait for this scene. Luckily, it's early on in the picture, and you can watch the peacock during the musical lead-up to the high note; I can't be sure, of course, but I could swear that bird knows what's coming.

FOR ALL HIS SOPHISTICATION, Vincente could be thrown for a loop when it came to the peculiarities of European everyday mechanics. French telephones, for example. It is certainly true that at the time of this story, thirty years ago, making a phone call in France was a philosophical experience. A possible comparison might have been finding a disused phone box in the swamps of rural Georgia, and attempting to make a call through the local operator to an outlying province in China.

At any rate, I found myself taking a pleasant and aimless walk in one of the suburbs of Paris—Neuilly, I think—when suddenly I heard my name called. I turned to find a distinctly distraught Vincente, whom I had not seen for a very long time. He was too nervous to bother with the amenities of a greeting. "André, you speak French, right?" Yes, I did. "Can you help me make a phone call? I can't even find a pay phone anywhere and this is an important call." I said I'd try to help, although pay phones outside central Paris are a dodgy business. We walked awhile and found one of those tiny cafés with two hissing coffee machines, a bar, and the requisite rusting football game in the center of the room. I asked the proprietor, a dead ringer for Raimu, whether he had a phone we could use. He put down his lunch, a garlic sandwich on garlic bread, wiped his hands, and brought out a key with which he unlocked a cubicle in the back of the bar. I bought a *jeton,* those odd tokens which are fed into French phones, got the operator on the line, and asked Vincente what number he wanted. He produced a slip of paper and gave it to me.

"Here," he said matter-of-factly, "I want to call, collect, Abe Lastvogel, and he's staying at this number in Vegas." I found this hard to take in. "You mean you think you're going to call Las Vegas right now from right here?" I asked. Vincente nodded impatiently. I tried to reason with him. "Vincente, if you go back to your hotel, give the operator downstairs this number, tell her it's absolutely vital, go to your room and don't move for twenty-four hours, you might, and I repeat *might,* get through."

Vincente's French was extremely patchy. He was married to a gorgeous French girl, but their communication could not have been verbal. When he was shooting *Gigi* in the Bois de Boulogne in 1959, he wanted two dozen black swans to swim picturesquely on the small lake. The unit manager of the production—the man who takes care of all possible details—was an experienced, very professional Frenchman named Serge. On this particular day Vincente decided to make his wishes known in Serge's own language. Unfortunately, his vocabulary got the better of him and he mistook the word *singe* ("monkey") for *cygne* ("swan"). Serge, by this time, had learned to accept the American film unit's wishes with total stoicism. His was not to question, right? The director wanted two dozen black monkeys on the lake tomorrow morning, *zut alors,* why not indeed? He trotted off on his interesting mission. The next morning, with just a hint of pride in his efficiency, he announced, "Monsieur Minnelli, the twenty-four monkeys are here."

Vincente's mouth began to twitch slightly, always a danger sign. "Monkeys? Monkeys?" he asked, his voice rising up the scale. "What bloody monkeys?" It took rather a long time to straighten out the misunderstanding, and much shouting. At last, the mystery cleared up, Serge tried to explain that black swans were at a premium in Paris. Indeed he did not know of any, but had heard that one of the French cabinet ministers bred black swans at his country estate for a hobby. "Well," announced Vincente, "get me those then," and he turned to go back to the camera.

What particular methods of persuasion Serge employed is not known to me, but believe it or not, there they were the next morning, floating serenely and smoothly on the lake, patrician cabinet minister birds to the core. Serge confided to me that it had been a true diplomatic feat to persuade the minister to part with his valuable birds even for one day, and veiled promises and threats had been made on both sides. Vincente wandered over to the edge of the lake. "Aren't they beautiful, Monsieur Minnelli?" Serge asked proudly.

Vincente had already turned away. "Not black enough," he threw over his shoulder, and climbed up onto the boom.

GIGI WAS A DREAM of an assignment. First and foremost, the film was lovely and intelligent, with a delicious story by Colette and terrific songs by Lerner and Loewe. Second, I was sent to Paris for the preproduction work. Originally I was told to expect a stay of four to six weeks; however, the film editor, Adrienne Fazan, who was an old hand at location work on a big musical, gave me some solid advice. "Take enough stuff and be prepared," she said. "I bet the schedule will be several weeks longer."

Well, she had guessed conservatively. I spent a total of thirteen weeks in Paris, on salary, all expenses picked up by the studio. I was young, I had no responsibilities or emotional ties, it was, in short, paradisaical. The work wasn't all that easy, but it did not consume all the hours of every day and I had probably the last completely carefree time of my life.

One Saturday afternoon, Arthur Freed informed me that I would have to spend Sunday in the sound department of Poste Parisienne, a recording studio on the Champs-Elysées, preparing the tracks and records of a number that had suddenly been rescheduled to shoot the following Monday. It would be the work of many hours and I was sorry to have to phone our French dubbing mixer Jean-Claude with news that would spoil his weekend.

I had not counted on Jean-Claude's independence.

"Ah, I'm really sorry," he said, "but I can't work tomorrow, I promised my girl that I would take her for lunch in the country."

I was the brainwashed product of years at MGM. "You don't understand," I explained. "You're working for the studio and they need this stuff Monday. We'll just have to get it done."

Jean-Claude was charming but immovable. "No, no, my friend," he insisted, "I am aware that I will be paid double time for a Sunday, but I have already been on double time a great deal on this film, and I don't need any more right now. I will take my girl to the country for lunch."

I began to be amused, but not too much. I laid out the facts for him: A big Hollywood studio would not recognize his decision as a valid one, he might come in for quite a bit of trouble, they tended to be peculiar about schedules on location, and so on and on. He listened with sympathy. "I don't want to let you down, so I tell you what I will be happy to do. Tomorrow morning, if the weather is bad, I will meet you at the sound studio at ten o'clock and we'll work. But if the sun is shining, I will ask my girl to bring along a friend for you and we will pick you up at the hotel at nine-thirty." By this time I realized I was tilting at windmills and I stopped arguing. In the morning I drew the curtains and saw brilliant sunshine. Jean-Claude and his lady hooted the horn for me at nine-thirty. His car had the top down; he had brought along a perfectly charming girl for me; there was a basket of food and several bottles of wine in the back; and we drove off to have a memorably nice day. I don't think either of us mentioned the work at all.

Come Monday morning, Minnelli and Freed had changed their minds, the schedule had been altered again, and I was told that the number in question would not shoot for another five days. Jean-Claude was perfectly relaxed. "I told you," he said, smiling. "You must learn to give preference to the important things in life!"

Ascribed to an individual's thinking process, the story is sweet. On the other hand, when this attitude was applied to daily life on the set, it drove those of us with American work habits up the wall. For instance, we were scheduled to record several songs in August, and no one had remembered that everyone leaves Paris in August for their annual vacation. I mean *everyone*. Have you ever tried to send out laundry in Paris in August? Or get a car repaired, or a pipe installed, or a wall painted? Well, it can't be done, not for anything. *Les vacances* are sacred and immovable.

I tried getting together an orchestra and failed miserably. I went down to the opera and to the Orchestre National, and gave stirring speeches. I did everything but recall the Lafayette Escadrille and the French and Indian Wars in order to garner sympathy and help, but it was very slim pickings. A handful of backstand players, obviously deeply in debt, were willing to sell out to the Ugly American, but far from the necessary number.

One night, a few days before the first scheduled recording, I was having a couple of drinks in a new club, with Louis Jourdan one of the stars of the film. There was a floor show: the customary ghastly singer, a line of chorus girls bored with the fact that they were nearly naked, and a helter-skelter band accompanying the acts. I suddenly began to pay attention to the music. The band was desultory, to be sure, but the bass player! A true virtuoso, a terrific player in an otherwise dismal group. The show finished, and the owner of the club came to our table, obsequious and anxious to please so big a movie star as Louis.

"Anything in the show you or your friend like?" he asked, leering and nudging the air. I was hot on the trail of a badly needed addition to our orchestra.

"The bass player!" I said excitedly. "Can you get me the bass player?"

The club owner was taken aback, but only for a moment. "I

don't know about that, monsieur," he stalled politely, "I'd have to ask him first."

It wasn't until I realized that Louis was trying not to fall off his chair with suppressed laughter that I came to grips with the magnitude of the misunderstanding. Turning the color of a tomato with high blood pressure, and talking at the speed of a basketball announcer, I offered my explanation and assured the skeptical owner that what I *really* wanted was to take the entire chorus line to Tahiti for the weekend. The bass player? Well, he turned out to be one of France's best-known jazz players, Pierre Michelot, and I worked with him many times after that. But not on *Gigi;* naturally he, too, was leaving on *les vacances!*

It certainly cannot be claimed that *Gigi* was shot in a hurry. Schedules were shredded as soon as they were made, and on one occasion it took as long to get one number staged and photographed as it took to write, film, and release a thirteen-part serial at Republic Studios. Periodically a revised budget would be discussed on the set, and the unit manager was always easy to identify; he was the one in sack cloth, kneeling in a darkened corner of the sound stage, rubbing ashes on his brow and smiting his forehead with large, theatrical gestures.

These delays in the schedule reached a kind of zenith in the sequence to be shot in the Palais de Glace, an ice skating rink that had been redecorated by Cecil Beaton at his most flamboyant. The scene in question involved the following: Louis Jourdan and Leslie Caron were to sit watching hundreds of ice skating couples waltzing dreamily to the strains of Lerner and Loewe, when Eva Gabor, playing Louis's discarded lover, would come up to the spectators' railing to speak to him. At this point, her new boy friend, in a flurry of ice spray, was to skate over at great speed and come to an impressive and instant athletic stop in order to stake his claim. The young man hired to play this part was a French professional skater. He had charm, he was nice-looking, and he could certainly skate, but when he opened his mouth to speak, he was a dead loss. Minnelli spent a downhill morning trying to inject some life into the young man, but it would have been easier to get a performance out of Rex the Wonder Horse. Arthur Freed had wandered down to the set and he watched with growing disbelief. Finally he asserted himself. "Fire him, Vincente," he said. "Pay him off and fire him."

Vincente was worried; where would he get an instant replacement? After all, hundreds of extras, all in period Beaton costumes, would be standing around waiting and getting paid, together with an enormous crew. Never mind, this was a class production—cancel the rest of the day and we'll find a perfect understudy. This was announced to one and all, and with a certain amount of Gallic shrugging, the set was cleared for the day. By the next morning, despite nonstop importuning of actors and agents, no one even vaguely suitable had been found.

"Better hire that kid again, Vincente," Arthur said. "We gotta get this shot." Vincente's nerves, always fragile, were fraying visibly. The French skater was found and, sensing a good moment, asked for considerably more money than before, which was of course granted with only a modicum of threatening abuse. Filming was resumed, the hundred couples waltzed, Eva Gabor managed her dialogue, and the skating beau whizzed to a virile halt, inches from the railing. At which point he forgot his lines, not once, not twice, but again and again.

Freed's patience snapped. "Fire him, Vincente," he announced imperiously, "and close down: we'll just have to find somebody else somewhere."

The previous day's farce was repeated once more, and everyone went home. Now the MGM production department went into overdrive. They found that a French actor named Jacques Bergerac was shooting a picture on the Riviera. He was tall and good-looking and had played a certain number of parts in Hollywood. It had been said that he couldn't act his way out of a paper bag, but he had scornfully disproved that by acting his way out of a paper bag, in public. Mr. Bergerac now had to be bribed to leave the production he was in and join *Gigi*. The money offered was evidently persuasive, along with the promise of very prominent billing, so a private plane was dispatched to Nice to bring our missing ice skater to Paris for the next day's shooting.

He arrived on the evening before and was greeted with understandable enthusiasm by one and all. There was a small snag left, but it could be managed—Mr. Bergerac was considerably taller than our hapless previous boy, and all the costumes would have to be remade overnight. The calls went out, a platoon of seamstresses came in, and the needles flew. The great day dawned. The set was lighted. The dancers danced, the orchestra played. Jacques showed up in costume, looking great, and a full rehearsal was under way. Vincente sat under the camera boom, watching.

"Now, Jacques, now," he shouted, "skate over to Miss Gabor as fast as you can and come to a quick stop!!!"

Jacques was completely taken aback.

"Skate?" he asked, bewildered and petulant. "Skate? I can't ice-skate! No one ever mentioned that I had to skate!"

Poor Vincente. He began to twitch like a seismograph needle just before the California Big One. "Cut!" he screamed. "Cut! Christ Almighty! Get the other kid back! Dismiss the set!"

In the ensuing confusion, a certain number of cooler heads prevailed. Jacques would be taught how to skate that day, and by tomorrow he would rival Robin Cousins, surely that could be done, no? Well, it turned out that the answer was a resounding *no.* Jacques couldn't even stand up on the ice, much less spray to an elegant stop. At last, Vincente, who looked by now as if he had been cast in a large Jell-O mold, made a decision.

"Forget it," he twitched. "I won't show his feet and I won't show him full figure, put two good skaters on either side of him and have them shove him along the ice just on his shoes." And that, lovers of cinema verité, is exactly what happened. What's more, it didn't look bad. And it only took four days to cross that expanse of ice; probably no more time than it took Eisenstein to shoot the Battle on the Ice in *Alexander Nevsky.*

FIVE

WHEN I RETURNED to Los Angeles in 1985 as the music director of the Los Angeles Philharmonic, it was after a twenty-two-year
absence from the city. I had gone to England in the mid-sixties and
had not set foot in a studio in all those intervening years. I was
amazed to find enormous changes, a much greater emphasis on the
visual arts, a less bizarre architectural medley, and a marked rise in a
cosmopolitan outlook.

However, certain habits in the film capital die hard. A few
months after my arrival, the town geared itself for the upcoming
annual Academy Awards, and the time warp took over. The same
slavering advertisements appeared, the same self-serving plugs and
interviews, and above all, the same self-delusion that the entire
world was waiting with bated breath to see who would be nominated in every category. The harsh truth is of course that no one
remembers who last year's winners were, nor do they care. It is true
that millions and millions of viewers watch the telecast of the
awards ceremony, and that some of the audience actually stays
awake right to the end, but the same can be said for the Miss
America Pageant, and how many Miss North Dakotas of the past
can you name?

During the period of my life with which this book is concerned,
I was quite involved with the Awards, having been nominated more
than a dozen times and having actually won an Oscar on four occasions, for *Gigi, Irma la Douce, Porgy and Bess,* and *My Fair Lady.* No
matter how critical I appear right now, it must be admitted that

while I was in the thick of things I was just as brainwashed as the rest of the town and spent a ludicrous amount of time speculating about the little statuettes. Who would win for best black-and-white art direction, and supporting actress, and short subject? Were Reuters and Tass and the BBC standing by to flash the news to travelers on the Burma Road? It is virtually impossible to exaggerate the film industry's self-importance at this time of year; no Pulitzer, no mere Nobel, no knighthood, no ascendancy to the peerage could compete. Even during the less frantic seasons, the insularity of Los Angeles is amazing; beyond the borders of Burbank to the south and Culver City to the north, *nothing* is seen to be of importance. It makes life a good deal more sanguine, but it is of course the Twilight Zone.

During my fourteen years in the film industry, I attended five of the awards ceremonies in the audience, and another three as the conductor of the pit orchestra. It might be interesting to disclose how it is possible for the forty-piece orchestra to play the appropriate theme music every time a winner is announced, so that the overwhelmed recipient can stumble up on stage, accompanied by his or her very own melody. There are five nominations in every category, and therefore five apropos pieces of music. To prevent orchestral chaos following each disclosure of a winner, the five themes, labeled by the title of the film and with the name of the individual nominee, are reduced to an eight-bar loop, repeatable as many times as necessary, and copied onto a single page of music manuscript paper. Each member of the orchestra has his instrument's correct page in front of him. The envelope is opened, the name is read, and there is the inevitable scream of jubilation from the audience. This scream is all-pervasive for a few seconds, thus giving the orchestral players time to fix their gaze on the correct theme on the page, the conductor to give a downbeat, and the strains of the winning film's music to be played. It's all done very smoothly and quickly, thus giving rise to the theory that the winners are actually known in advance, because how else could the right tune be played? No, in fact, the secrecy of the winner's identity is scrupulously guarded, and the envelopes are probably kept on a nuclear submarine which surfaces backstage only in time for the show.

I know from practical experience, having won and lost several times, that there is no way to stay perfectly cool and above it all when the list of nominees is read. Maybe it would be easier at home, listening to the TV set, but when you are right there, reserve and common sense are put into a hammerlock by adrenaline, and for that one minute *You wanna win, you wanna win!!* Of course it's nonsense, of course it's like Prize Day at school, but as Mike Nichols observed with typical candor, "If you're in any contest at all where you can win or lose, try to win." It's true.

The rules and bylaws of the Academy, perhaps cognizant of the fact that the general audience cares only about the actors, decree that a great many of the other categories are lumped together as "Technical Awards." The music awards are filed under "Technical," a misconception that has enraged a great many composers. For some churlish reason Aaron Copland, Erich Korngold, Miklós Rózsa, Bernard Herrmann, David Raksin and others don't consider themselves technicians rather than artists. Another quibble I might mention is the rule that every single member of the Academy, regardless of his individual branch, is allowed to vote on every category in the final ballot. I know I am not equipped to vote on the niceties and details governing the prize in set decoration or film editing, and conversely, I am not prepared to put too much credence in Sylvester Stallone's opinion on composition.

The show itself, at least in the theater, is usually a merciful blur. The nominees are in a haze except for those minutes concerned with their own category, and the nonconcerned spectators find out very quickly that it is a lot better to watch at home. Ennui is more easily dealt with, the overpowering urge to grab a short nap is not embarrassing in private, and getting dressed in evening clothes at five in the afternoon is either decadent or foolish. The most mysterious part of the show seems to be the opening song-and-dance number. With all the talent of the motion picture industry available and willing to contribute, why is it this number seems to be staged by the same people responsible for the Elks' Club Picnic in Fargo? What keeps the nominees in their seats, smiling stiffly, is the suspense of sweating out their eventual victory or loss. Once that moment has passed and rational standards return, it's a tough evening. When you win, collect the Oscar, and come off stage, you are requested to go to the press room for a session with the photographers. The first time it happened to me, I demurred and indicated that I should really return out front fairly quickly. Ella Fitzgerald was backstage and came over to me, beaming with friendship. "Don't be silly, honey," she said. "After all, how many times does this happen? Enjoy it, relax, have your picture taken!" "Okay, Ella," I said, "but I think your song is due next and I'm supposed to conduct for you." She had her arm around my shoulder and gave me a little squeeze. "Honey," she said again, "get the hell back in that pit!!"

The Oscars meant a lot to me at the time I won them. I was pleased and proud of them. Now that I view my film work from a distance, and across a wide gulf of the intervening years, they have taken on a different perspective—they have become three-dimensional objects of nostalgia. It is always a problem to know where to keep them. Too blatantly displayed is awful. A well-known actress had a niche built into the wall of her sitting room, and a pin spotlight concealed in the ceiling. When the light was on, it bathed her Oscar in a mysterious golden reflection, and one expected a healing spring to gurgle forth miraculously under the figurine. On the other hand, using Oscar as a door stop is bending over backward too far. I keep mine in the corner of a bookcase, where I like to think they are visible but not pushy.

A well-meaning friend suggested that the four prizes would be a daily invitation to complacency, but I can dissuade him of that notion by making reference to a different kind of statue. In the mid-seventies, a life-size figure of me was molded and put on display in Madame Tussaud's Wax Museum in London. As the model for this figure, I had to go to the Wax Museum, where the sculptor walked around and around me, taking Polaroid shots and measuring my head with calipers. Then, a case with many narrow drawers was wheeled in. I could not imagine what its dozens of drawers contained until the sculptor's assistant, having looked intently into my eyes, opened one of these drawers, which were the size and dimension of a large butterfly collection, and revealed that they were full of glass eyeballs. I tried to keep my composure by making trivial conversation. "This place has been open for a hundred years or more," I babbled. "Everyone is here, from Jack the Ripper to Solzhenitsyn, but what happens to the statues once the subject's fame, or infamy, runs its course? Do you ever get rid of them?" The sculptor frowned and thought. "No, not in my time," he said. "I can't remember it happening." His assistant, a personable young lady, looked up brightly. "No sir, excuse me, you're wrong about that," she chirped. "I can recall melting down Alan Ladd."

Well, kiddies, that's what I think about during moments of complacency.

They melted down Alan Ladd.

DURING MY YEARS in Hollywood actually no one would have grieved if many of the musicians' Oscars had been melted down. Composers were never regarded as members of the elite. The class system, according to history and literature, has always been most prevalent in England. I think the film studios of the era I am recalling ran the Empire a close second.

At the top of the heap were, of course, the studio bosses. Of the many I worked for, none was more fearsome than Jack Warner, the eponymous boss of Warner Brothers. Tough, dirty-talking, and beholden to no one, he struck terror into the hearts of actors and employees alike. He had gambled on a great many innovations and won, the most famous being the advent of talking pictures. He loved making speeches, most of them larded with such tactlessness and scatology as to turn his audiences into pillars of salt. Instead of promenading down the studio streets, as was L. B. Mayer's wont, Jack Warner strode purposefully. He would call out his greetings loudly and jovially, and they never varied from day to day. The writing team of Shavelson and Rose worked for him for many years. One day he encountered Jack Rose walking by himself. Warner still boomed out, "Hi, boys," unable to affix the singular to half of his team.

Somehow, he got it into his mind after our first meeting that I was French. He was the proud possessor of the Légion d'honneur, so he liked the idea. In 1963, I was at the studio for a year, working on *My Fair Lady* and a Bette Davis melodrama, and every single day, without exception, upon seeing me appear, Warner would bellow, "How are ya, monsewer," and this *bon mot* would be followed by loud barks of laughter. It may seem churlish of me, but it got to the point where my stomach would tighten into knots of apprehension, waiting for this hilarious joke, and I finally took to ducking into the nearest sound stage and hiding for a few minutes.

A greater law unto himself was Sam Goldwyn, for whom I worked for the better part of a year while I was music director on *Porgy and Bess.* Unlike other executives in Hollywood, he didn't just run a studio, he owned it, and in a curious way this simplified matters. When anyone needed a decision of any kind, whether it involved the size of an orchestra, the building of a set, or the prolonging of a schedule, Mr. Goldwyn was it. If the answer was yes, you went ahead; if it was no, you had to think of an alternative. There was no going to anyone else, no trying to convince a committee or a board of directors. Along with everyone else, I had enormous respect for him. However, I have to admit that I was hoping to hear my share of Goldwynisms, those fascinating manglings of syntax and vocabulary that have become legend. He didn't disappoint me. On the very first day at his studio, I was sitting in his office, together with the director who started (but did not finish) the film, Rouben Mamoulian. While we were waiting for the star, Sidney Poitier, to arrive, Rouben mentioned Mrs. Goldwyn's upcoming birthday.

"What are you giving her, Sam?" he asked.

The old gentleman looked at his wife's photo, which sat in a massive silver frame on his desk. "You know, Rouben, Frances has very beautiful hands. I've always been crazy about her hands. So this year, for her birthday, I'm having a bust made of them."

Halfway through the production of *Porgy and Bess,* Mr. Goldwyn was invited to come down to the large rehearsal hall in order to see the elaborate number Sammy Davis Jr. had been working on. Sammy played Sportin' Life, and his song "It Ain't Necessarily So" had been extended in order to give free reign to his talents as a dancer. I had seen a run-through earlier that day, in preparation for writing the arrangement, and had thought it a kind of impressive steamroller of a number, a superfinale, with nothing left out save possibly the Odessa steps and a parade of flags. Goldwyn walked in and sat down. Sammy ran over to him.

"Before we start, Mr. Goldwyn, I have something for you, a present."

Goldwyn was slightly bewildered. "Why a present, Sammy?"

Now I have to explain that Sammy was a present giver. He handed out gifts the way other people share their chewing gum. And these presents were elaborate—gleaming jewelry, extraordinary cameras, amazing clothing. On this occasion he produced an oblong jeweler's box and waited for Goldwyn to open it.

"See, it's a watch," he said, "heart-shaped. And on the back it says, 'To Sam from Sam' because I'm so grateful to you for giving me this dream part, Mr. Goldwyn. And look," he continued, warming to his narrative, "these buttons show you the time in other countries, this explains the phase of the moon, this one is a perpetual calendar, and this one is a stop watch down to hundredths of a second."

Goldwyn examined the watch with interest. "That's very nice, very nice indeed," he said. Sammy smiled, walked over to the set, and sprang into action, along with dozens of singers, dancers, and extras. "It Ain't Necessarily So" began. Sammy was never, shall we say, a laid-back performer; he liked to go right for the throat, and this number was a killer, even by his standards. At last, chorus after chorus spiraled to a climax, and on the last high note, Sammy jumped off a parapet, landed in what is known as a split, and did a spectacular knee slide that ended a couple of feet from where Goldwyn was watching. There was a moment's silence and then we heard a faint click. We all watched as Goldwyn studied his beautiful new present carefully.

"It's too long," he announced as he got to his feet, waved goodbye, and left the stage.

Sammy was still on his knees, covered with sweat and glory. Slowly he got up and dusted himself off.

"Can you believe it?" he asked of no one in particular. "I had to give the son of a bitch a stopwatch!!"

But we composers were definitely not of the elite and Madame Defarge knitted nothing for us when we went to the guillotine. We were a necessary cog in the wheel, like the people who made fake lawns and worked out how far Tarzan's vines had to swing. We were often put in our place by the more glamorous toilers, even the nonhuman ones.

Let me explain. One day there was a production meeting in Arthur Freed's offices. Present were Rouben Mamoulian, Fred Astaire, Irene Sharaff, Cyd Charisse, Freed, and myself. The day was blistering hot and we kept the doors to the corridor open. Lassie, beloved collie star, came panting down the hall, led by her trainer, a man whose name actually was Weatherwax. He looked inside our rooms and decided to show off his star. A few words into the dog's ear, *sotto voce,* and Lassie came in, walked over to Freed, sat up, and offered her paw in greeting, whereupon everyone chorused, "Isn't that wonderful?" Encouraged, the collie repeated the piece of business with Mr. Mamoulian, the director, swung over to Fred, and did not miss the ladies present. I was next in line on the sofa. Lassie came over, gave me a cool look of appraisal, turned, and wandered out. I had been snubbed by a dog act! Obviously it rankled since I still remember it.

Within the compartmentalized divisions of the hierarchy, there were differences as well. Years later, during the filming of *Irma la Douce* in Paris, it was extraordinary to see that the five-dollar ladies near the rue Madeline were dismissive and vicious about their two-dollar sisters in Les Halles. The same sort of superiority complex was allowed, and even nurtured within the ranks of contract writers and composers.

At Christmas time it was a tradition for presents to be given by directors, producers, and agents, and the recipients were carefully classified. Almost all the composers were represented by the same agency, MCA, and the gifts sent by this monolithic office were carefully chosen. Over the years I had graduated, courtesy of my Academy Awards, to one of the better lists, and had been sent some luggage one year, and a carriage clock the next.

It was on one of these occasions that a talented composer, Jeff Alexander, suddenly flew into a rage at being omitted. "Goddamnit, it's the principle of the thing," he snarled. "They take their commission from me, they can bloody well send me a present." Driven by anger, he actually phoned the MCA office and told them that he had been left out completely. Their apology was profuse. An oversight, a mistake, good heavens, would he be at the studio for another hour, the delivery van was on its way. Jeff was mollified. He speculated on his forthcoming present. Would it be a briefcase? A matching letter opener and magnifying glass? A case of wine? At last the delivery man knocked on his office door. "Happy Holidays," he sang and handed Jeff one pound of mixed nuts. Jeff actually had an interesting plan as to what he would do with these nuts, one by one, in the MCA offices, but we managed to dissuade him.

Still, relative peons like Jeff and me managed to find opportunities for assertions of independence.

Periodically the big studios, driven by guilt and fear, went on an economy drive. This usually resulted in the firing of a few secretaries and a futile attempt to inflict some stringent rules on the workday patterns of the employees. At Warner Brothers, Jack Warner issued the ukase that all writers had to check in at nine in the morning. Approximately a month later he sent for Julius Epstein, a marvelous screenwriter whose credits included *Casablanca*. "I just read your new script, Julie," he said, "and I've never read such unmitigated crap before in my life!"

Julie was bewildered. "But Mr. Warner, how is that possible? The script simply can't be bad. After all, I was here every morning at nine sharp!"

At Metro, in the music department, a similar rule was instigated by the department's bookkeeper and accountant, a Mr. I. M. Halperin, a pale man with rimless glasses and a rimless sense of humor. All composers, the rule stated, had to be on the lot between ten and six every day, and should there be a deviation from these hours, he had to be notified. The rule was posted, and we waited in vain for Zorro to come and make his mark on the memo. However, as it happened, I had to work straight through the night soon after, and when I finally tottered out of my office, with eyes red as a rabbit's, I noticed that it was four in the morning. I went back to my desk and rang Mr. I. M. Halperin at home. It took quite a few rings before he answered. "Hello," I said cheerfully, "I'm so sorry to bother you, but this is André. I've just finished work, it's not six in the evening, it's four in the morning, so I thought I had better let you know that I'm going home now." The rule was rescinded two days later, and for a very little while I was a folk hero.

All these attempts by executives to marshal the muse into line pale into insignificance in comparison to an edict once issued by Irving Thalberg.

He was the most renowned of all the MGM producers but his reign at the studio was in the early thirties, so I missed out working for him. He was the model for Scott Fitzgerald's *Last Tycoon,* and is generally held to have been an awesome figure of intellect, taste, and drive, and the old-timers in Hollywood still speak of him as a sort of combination Ziegfeld and Teilhard de Chardin. It is entirely possible that he was a beacon of enlightenment, but when it came to music his fund of information was minuscule. One day, the story goes, he was in his projection room running a new MGM film when something on the sound track bothered him. "What is that?" he asked irritably into the darkness. "What is that in the music? It's awful, I hate it!"

The edge in his voice required an answer, even if that answer was untainted by knowledge. One of his minions leapt forward. "That's a minor chord, Mr. Thalberg," he offered. The next day, an inter-office memo arrived in the music department with instructions to post it conspicuously. It read as follows: "From the above date onward, no music in an MGM film is to contain a 'minor chord.'" Signed, "IRVING THALBERG." When I left the studio for the last time, twenty-five years after this missive's arrival, it was still on the wall in the music department, under glass and heavily bolted. I must now confess that I actually tried to get the thing off the wall with a heavy-duty screwdriver, but nothing would budge the rusted screws. Maybe there would have been a curse attached to it, and I would have been doomed to spend eternity in a projection room, running and rerunning Norma Shearer in *Marie Antoinette.*

SIX

THE TRUTH IS that I was nothing more exalted than a craftsman —and the people I came to cherish and respect the most in my Hollywood years were all consummate masters of their craft.

It is always easier to write a bad review than a good one. It is always easier to deride a performance than to praise it. By the same standards it is infinitely funnier to recount Hollywood stories that are all about incompetents, illiterates, and phonies. God knows there was a cast of thousands of them, but there were always artists and technicians of enormous talents, artistic integrity, and amazing knowledge. In the years I spent in the film business, every studio had a music department with contract composers, arrangers, librarians and copyists. Also, every studio had its own contract orchestra of approximately seventy-five players. These were musicians whose provenance included the world's great symphony orchestras and America's best dance bands.

It has often been remarked that the sight-reading ability of these orchestras was legendary, and I have to add my voice to that existing chorus. These players were genuinely amazing. They would show up each morning, utterly unaware of what it was they were expected to record that day. It could have been a score by Alex North or Bernard Herrmann or David Raksin or Miklós Rózsa, or just as easily, a Tom and Jerry cartoon or a dance number for Fred Astaire. They would casually glance at the parts on their stands, the ink still wet, and would proceed to play with the same expert disdain a professional parking lot attendant uses to back a new convertible into a tight space. It was a daily exhibition of the highest technical proficiency, and no one who witnessed it will ever forget it or disclaim it. The fact that the music might have been second-rate, or even tenth-rate, had no bearing on its degree of difficulty, but I never saw any of these instrumentalists come unglued. I suppose the closest to their particular talents are the various symphony orchestras in London, whose schedules are a combination of over-work and ridiculously low salaries, thus making it imperative that as little time is spent on rehearsals as humanly possible. I remember that in the fifties, MGM had under contract fourteen composers, approximately ten orchestrators, and a room full of copyists permanently bent over desks, squinting under Dickensian eye shades. Now, at the time of this writing, no studio has any musicians of any kind, writing or playing, under contract. Quite a change.

The orchestrators were my first, and probably my closest, friends. At MGM alone there were Conrad Salinger, Bob Franklyn, Al Woodbury, Sandy Courage, Leo Arnaud, and Ted Duncan—not a household name among them but every one of them schooled to a real perfection of his craft. Often they were saddled with the problem of making the scrawls or verbal wishes of *soi-disant* composers into something glamorous and wonderful, and so it was necessary for them to have the maximum of expertise and the minimum of conceit. It is a source of great pride to me that I was a member of this incognito band for a while.

I have a vivid memory of Al Woodbury filling page after page of the giant yellow score pads while avidly listening to the ball game on the radio, and never missing a note or mistaking a clef or a transposition. One night I had been working terribly late, two in the morning, and as I made my stumbling way out of the studio and toward the parking lot, I noticed Bob Franklyn's cubbyhole office still lit. I stuck my head in and there was Bob, meticulously orchestrating someone's music in his elegant French-schooled manner, yawning luxuriously and peering up at me over his rimless glasses. We chatted for a few minutes, competing as to who had the worse assignment, when a gust of wind from the open window blew the page Bob was working on from his desk onto the floor. Now, it must be explained at this point that a page of score for full orchestra consists of about thirty-two staves, four bars per stave, and that this particular page was almost completely filled in Bob's fine hand. For the normal, talented composer, it would represent several hours of hard work. Bob looked at the page on the floor a full six feet away, and thought about physical effort versus mental application. He sighed and picked up a brand new page from the ream of paper by his side.

"The hell with it," he said and started over, the pencil gliding effortlessly over the woodwind parts.

All of us were expected to be total chameleons. "I want this to sound like . . ." Fill in the name of your preference: Ravel, Tchaikovsky, Strauss, Count Basie, a Broadway pit; that was an instruction we all heard, many times during working hours, and we were expected to nod submissively, go away, and produce the musical goods. I was never in the pantheon of Hollywood orchestrators, but I learned a lot and was able to put it to use for the rest of my life. Don't let anyone mistake these gentlemen's unquestioning music habits as hack work; any examination of their scores would prove the most enviable, sophisticated knowledge of what makes an orchestra sound.

Naturally, some of the composers were more capable of doing their own orchestrating. My point of view has always been that, given the hair-raising shortness of time allotted to the completion of a score, if help is needed, then that is fair dues. On the other hand, if orchestrating help is sought by a composer because he doesn't know how, then that is meretricious.

When Aaron Copland wrote music to *The Red Pony,* his detailed sketches were scored by a staff orchestrator at the studio. A colleague of Copland's, shocked by the disclosure of this weakness, asked Aaron how he could allow such a thing. Aaron produced a page of his handwritten sketch. "Look at this," he said, "and answer me the following: If I dictate a letter and it is typed for me, who actually wrote the letter, me or my secretary?"

It's a valid point, but only if the composer's sketch, or short score, is as complete as Copland's obviously was. I orchestrated for Hugo Friedhofer once. Hugo, in his early days, had scored the music for Korngold and Steiner, and there was nothing about the orchestra he didn't know. His sketch could have been handed right to a copyist, and I felt as if I were stealing as I translated his dots onto individual lines on the big pages. There was nothing left for me to do except the wearying mechanics of it all. Hugo was a sensational musician, capable of being moved to tears by music, and just as capable of some of the most ribald and awful jokes extant.

He also kept his individuality. He once composed the music to a Western; in the projection room, the producer was baffled. "Hugo," he demanded, "your music for the villains is, if anything, more heroic than for the hero! Why did you do that?" Hugo was sanguine. "I liked them," he explained.

It isn't just actors who get typed in a specific mold. Composers suffer the same fate. I had done some successful musicals; therefore, I was the one to get for a musical. Then I did four of Billy Wilder's comedies in a row and I became the comedy expert. After I did "Elmer Gantry," every script that was tough and uncompromising came my way. Producers love pigeonholing everybody; it makes assigning and casting so much easier.

Miklós Rózsa is one of the film world's most famous and prestigious composers. When I knew him at Metro, he was knee-deep in his religious phase. *Quo Vadis?, King of Kings, Barabbas, Ben Hur*— he did 'em all. As soon as there were actors in sight wearing white robes and sandals, poor Miklós was called. These were tough films to compose, if for no other reason than the fact that they were absolutely crammed with music, wall-to-wall pious *tuttis,* and it must have been wildly boring for someone of Miklós's standing.

Once I saw him come out of a projection room really in despair.

"I just don't know what else to write for that scene in which that fella carries the cross up that hill," he complained. This might not have been Bach's problem, but for lesser mortals, it was a genuine challenge. In order to keep himself interested, Miklós did an amazing (and probably unnecessary) amount of research for each of his projects, and so he was a real expert in biblical instruments, plainsong, Gregorian chant, and the like. He was, in other words, a scholar, and an anachronism in Culver City. During *Ben Hur,* he was beside himself with impotent rage when the director, William Wyler, suggested that "Silent Night, Holy Night" be played during the Nativity scene.

Poor Miklós: he was always the most European of gentlemen,

and his dark suits in the blazing sunshine typified how out of place he was.

THERE HAVE ALWAYS BEEN serious composers involved in film work. It is held in much higher esteem in Europe than it is in the United States, and some truly important names have been found on the credits of non-American films. William Walton, whose music for Laurence Olivier's Shakespeare films is among the best ever written for a movie, loved composing movie scores. Along with other British luminaries such as Vaughan Williams and Benjamin Britten, he felt that the tailoring of music to existing images was rewarding, not just financially but artistically. Sir William was a laconic creature, soft-spoken and slightly wicked, all of which cloaked a huge streak of sentimentality. I conducted and recorded a great deal of his symphonic output, and we were friends, a fact of which I am proud. One of my prize possessions is a page of orchestral manuscript which contains the beginning of what was to be his Third Symphony, and which he sent me for my birthday a few years ago. One day he called me with an unexpected question: "Who is Ron Goodwin?" he asked. It was not the sort of inquiry I expected from Sir William Walton.

"I can tell you, but I can't imagine why you want to know," I told him. "Ron Goodwin is a film composer; as a matter of fact, he was brought in to rewrite a score of mine when the producer didn't like my efforts."

Walton giggled. "What a nice coincidence," he said. "Mr. Goodwin has just been hired to rewrite my score to the film *Battle of Britain* because the producers didn't like *my* work!"

I was speechless. My train of thought was interrupted by Walton, this time with a very typical comment. "Tell me, old boy," he said. "Does this gent just rewrite music, or does he also write music?"

Even a cursory glance at the European films of the last fifty years will prove that a sizable amount of their music was written by Shostakovich, Prokofiev, Honegger, Sir Arthur Bliss, and Richard Rodney Bennett, and none of them were derided for turning their efforts to occasional film composing. In the United States, the attitude is different. Music critics have made it quite clear that any composer who ever contributed a four-bar jingle to a film was to be referred to as a "Hollywood composer" from then on, even if the rest of his output were to consist solely of liturgical organ sonatas.

Perhaps the only major American composer to beat this rap was Aaron Copland, whose scores for *Of Mice and Men, The Red Pony,* and *The Heiress* elevated those films by a considerable notch. However, even this dean of American composers had his title music for *Heiress* rewritten by a contract studio orchestrator, and it is fascinating to listen to this film when it surfaces on television. It begins with music under the credits; music that is slick, pretty, and utterly vapid. Then, suddenly, approximately two minutes along, there is a gear shift, and Copland's music takes over, spare and angular and gorgeous. It's like suddenly finding a diamond in a can of Heinz beans. Of course, Copland's influence on film music is immeasurable. His ballets *Appalachian Spring, Billy the Kid,* and *Rodeo* have left an ineradicable impression on a whole generation of composers, and I doubt whether any film composer faced with pictures of the Great American Outdoors, or any Western story, has been able to withstand the lure of trying to imitate some aspects of Copland's peculiar and personal harmony. Just as Elgar seems to spell "England" to the minds of most listeners, Copland *is* the American sound.

Erich Wolfgang Korngold was a master film composer. His wonderful melodies, orchestrated in the most gorgeous Richard Strauss–oriented manner, are a joy to hear, even when the films are forgettable. *Robin Hood, The Sea Hawk,* and *Elizabeth and Essex* all display Korngold's musical extravertism, and for some reason, his unmistakably Viennese kind of sentiment helped Errol Flynn be a convincing English hero. Korngold had been a genuine child prodigy, the real McCoy, compared when he was a child to no less than Mozart. He had operas and ballets performed in Vienna, by conductors such as Bruno Walter, before he reached his teens. He wrote chamber music, concertos, orchestral works, and a lengthy symphony, but once he had taken up residence at Warner Brothers Studios, in Burbank, California, he was forever branded a Hollywood composer. He was another man gifted with the ability to give a razor-sharp answer. Toward the end of his life, he ran into Max Steiner, another film composer, on the Warner Brothers street. They greeted each other, and then Max tried the opening gambit:

"You know, Erich, we've both been here at Warners for over twenty years," he said, "and something occurred to me recently; your music is slowly getting hackneyed, and mine is getting better!"

Korngold was unperturbed. "But the explanation is simple, Maxie," he purred. "I'm beginning to imitate you, and you're beginning to imitate me!"

A fascinating character in the days I was getting started in Hollywood was Bernard Herrmann. He had done illustrious work in the radio days of CBS, composing, and conducting out-of-the-way music few people had bothered with. He had written an opera, *Wuthering Heights,* and a symphony, and had then made his national mark by being Orson Welles's court composer, having written all the music for the Mercury Theatre productions, and subsequently the film scores to *Citizen Kane* and *The Magnificent Ambersons.* He was a musician gifted with inspiration and flawless craftsmanship. He was a walking encyclopedia of arcane music. The only word I can think of to adequately describe Benny's personality is the disused term "curmudgeon." He never tried to please or ingratiate, and he nearly always mistrusted and snarled. During any conversation with him, you had to prepare yourself for accusations and resentment, voiced in a high pitch of anger, an anger not arrived at by means of a gradual, normal *crescendo* of passion, but an anger exploding out of nothing and from nowhere. He telephoned me one morning. "You know the series I'm conducting at the museum," he began. "Well, I want you to play the C. P. E. Bach Piano Concerto with me, but I don't suppose you play it, nah, you don't know stuff like that, what's the matter, too busy working on junk? I don't imagine you'd be interested, the music's too special for you, right?"

I managed to stem the flow of invective long enough to speak, but I made the ultimate error. I said that I hadn't ever heard the particular piece he was referring to.

Bang! went Benny's adrenaline, and his voice was instantly apoplectic, went five whole tones up in pitch, Nero sentencing a recalcitrant slave: "Oh, that figures, never bothered, eh, typical, typical, Jesus, what a mentality, you probably never even heard of the composer, I don't know why I bother—"

I interrupted him by screaming into the phone, "I'll get the music, I'll get it today, I'll learn it within a week, I'll play it at the museum, what are you yelling about?" Benny seemed mollified for a second. "Well, okay," he mumbled into the receiver. But then his nature reasserted itself: "I'll take a bet you won't really do it, but we'll see, we'll see!!"

We all put up with Benny and his outrageous behavior; we all placated him and tried to step on the fuse that seemed permanently lit and sizzling toward his brain, because ultimately he was worth it. A remarkable musician. Many years after the incident I just related, he came to visit a recording session of mine in London, with the London Symphony. We were both living in England by then, and I can only guess that I had risen in Benny's estimation by leaving Hollywood and becoming a 52-week-a-year conductor, because he was soft-spoken and pleasant, and eager to have a normal conversation about the debatable missing cornet part in Berlioz's *Symphonie Fantastique*. It was as close to small talk as he could manage.

To get back to my friend Miklós Rózsa: Miklós had realized early on that it did no good to attempt writing serious music while residing in Hollywood. The blandishments of producers and the seduction of the weather were too omnipresent, so he would take himself off to his house in Italy, for approximately half the year. There he wrote his concert music, pottered around galleries looking for old drawings, and read innumerable books about music, in four languages. After six months of this, he would have finished a new work of some size, and refreshed his soul. I would see him upon his return, strolling down the scorching concrete streets of the studio, looking for all the world like someone in search of a shady sidewalk café in which to while away a few hours. One time I asked him whether he had met a new young composer about whom there had been a lot of talk.

Miklós made a gesture of dismissal. "Yes, yes," he shrugged, "but he's not serious. I looked at one of his scores in the library, and he doesn't even know that the plural of 'viola' is 'vio*le*' and not 'violas'!"

He made another small gesture of despair, a very Central European gesture, a man resigned to the fact that the *espresso* is not what it used to be. And then he went off, toward one of the sound stages, probably to argue about the merits of music with a producer who liked Mantovani.

Miklós befriended me when I was extremely callow, conducted for me on a few occasions when I was a piano soloist, extolled the virtues of having a second home in Europe, and warned me against getting too firmly entrenched in the film business. His Violin Concerto was written for Jascha Heifetz and his Viola Concerto for Pinchas Zuckerman. I conducted quite a lot of his music in later years, both in America and in Europe, and my admiration for his musicianship is enormous.

But back to those old days: In the early fifties I wrote some big band jazz for Miklós when he composed the score to John Huston's *Asphalt Jungle,* for the simple reason that Miklós asked for my help. His musicological education was vast, but I think the last time he had heard a dance band was in a tearoom in Budapest. Around that same time, he made a momentous, California-type decision: he would add a swimming pool to his Hollywood home. His house was in the hills, and built on a fairly steep bluff. However, he owned a sizable plot which could be reached by precipitously clambering down an incline from the main house. That was where Miklós wanted the pool, private and shady.

Well, the excavation was done and the cement-mixing truck followed. Miklós watched the cement for the foundation being prepared and was mentally already picking out the color of the beach umbrellas. However, there was to be a slight hitch. The cement mixer's brakes slipped and it plummeted down the hills and into the hole that was to be the pool's home. There the truck landed on its side and the driver yelled for help. The other workmen sprang into action, and the unfortunate man was pried out of the vehicle and taken off to the hospital with a badly sprained arm. Obviously, all work was postponed until the next day.

Come the next morning, a pretty sight greeted Miklós's eyes: some of the cement had run out of the truck and had firmly and permanently affixed the vehicle, on its side, to the excavation. Poor Miklós, it was not a situation he could identify with—these things don't happen on the Pusta, and he was beside himself. For the *coup de grâce,* the trucking company informed him that their wreck would have to be blasted loose, and work on his pool would then have to start all over again. I gave him an idea, which for some straitlaced reason, he rejected out of hand.

"Forget doing it again," I counseled. "Fill the damned thing with water. Invite your guests. Urge them to have a good time. But warn them that when they jump in, they must be careful. There's a truck cemented to the bottom of the pool."

DAVID RAKSIN is another West Coast musician whose knowledge is encyclopedic. He, too, grew restive with life under the palm trees, and took up a teaching position at the University of Southern California. His sense of orchestral color was always unbeatable, his harmonic twists very clearly his own, and he thought nothing of setting himself some problems to make studio composing a little livelier. He wrote fugues for Al Capone and twelve-tone sequences for cowboy heroes, but where he truly shone was in his invention of superb, melting melodies. "Laura" became world famous, of course, but some of his other tunes—"Separate Tables," "Slowly," and "Sylvia"—are just as lush.

My personal favorite is the extended and complicated theme he devised for *The Bad and the Beautiful,* Vincente Minnelli's elegant look at Hollywood folk. I was in my office struggling with some timings for *Above and Beyond* when David stuck his head in and asked whether I would listen to the main theme he had just finished for the Minnelli picture. I gladly made room at the piano and David demonstrated the tune. My heart sank. It was confused and confusing, the harmonies tumbled over one another, and the melody was a snake. I seem to remember that my disappointment was not masked very well, and David must have been hurt.

It wasn't until I visited him on the recording stage when the orchestra was playing the very same melody that I could put together what had happened. David is actually a pretty good pianist, but when playing his own tunes (especially a new one), he is so overcome by diffidence, by Oh-I-know-this-isn't-much, that he plays everything three times too quickly, with the sustaining pedal firmly anchored to the floor. Now, played stately and romantically, the theme was gorgeous and enviable.

David has always been part of the serious music contingent in Los Angeles. He was a personal friend of both Stravinsky and

Schoenberg and is currently close to many of the brighter composing lights on the West Coast. Quite recently he sent me a program
he had found for a modern music series in 1950, in which I was
listed as the pianist of the Jolivet Piano Concerto and the conductor of Boris Blacher's chamber opera *Romeo and Juliet,* along with a
note reminding me that he had attended all the rehearsals as well as
the performances. Now, over forty years later, he still shows up at
my Philharmonic rehearsals, and if it is a new work, he sits in the
stalls with a borrowed score, listening carefully and analytically. In
the spring of 1990, when Mel Powell won the Pulitzer Prize for his
Two-Piano Concerto, it was David who organized a celebratory
dinner for Mel.

Which brings me to another musician whose friendship has
weathered all the changes and vicissitudes. When I first heard Mel
Powell play, I was still a teenager and he was Benny Goodman's
famous pianist. I idolized his playing and tried copying his inven-
tions, which did me absolutely no good, since reproductions aren't
any better for music than they are for furniture or drawings.

Some years later, Mel became the orchestra pianist at MGM and
we began to spend quite a bit of time together, both professionally
and socially. I can remember Mel at the piano, earphones clamped
on, eyes glued to the screen, playing long glissandos down the
keyboard to match Jerry, the cartoon mouse, sliding down a cur-
tain. Another time he and I sat at two enormous Steinways blasting
through Miklós Rózsa's waltz from *Madame Bovary.* It was a nice
piece, dramatic and effective, but the film's director, Vincente Minnelli, and his wife Judy Garland went into such alarming ecstasies,
jumping up and down and weeping that it was "twice as good as
Ravel's 'La Valse,'" that Mel and I, along with the shocked composer, could hardly speak.

Mel, being a firm East Coast denizen, missed the snow around
winter time, and did a little research into its local availability. It
wasn't too difficult to find, and we rented a large cabin in the
woods in an area called Big Bear. This was a haven for recluses and
a mecca for cross-country skiers—glorious trees and nary a soul for
miles on end.

The cabin we had procured was wooden and drafty, and Mel and
I decided that a big, friendly fire blazing in the fireplace would be

just the ticket. We found, to our dismay, that all the logs piled outside the cabin in handy snowdrifts were too wet to light. I found a bottle of coal oil. Just the thing, Mel figured. We splashed some of the contents onto the damp wood. "Come on, come on," said Mel impatiently, "it isn't perfume, never mind just behind the earlobes," and carried away by our outdoorsmanship, we, the two big-city forest rangers, emptied the entire quart into the fireplace. Being afflicted not only with idiocy but also with fortunate coward-ice, we stood in the middle of the cabin and flicked a lit kitchen match onto the hearth.

Once the owner of the cabin, two visitors from nearby, and a passel of Boy Scouts had put out the fire, we hastened to assure our landlord that we would certainly replace the charred mess that had once passed for a wall. But we weren't finished proving ourselves as Mounties.

By the next evening we had become starved for music; the absence of it had made us extremely nervous. In a tool shed that belonged to the complex of rented cabins, we spied an ancient upright piano moldering in a corner under an onslaught of sleds and shovels. We dragged the cover off it and opened the lid. A few hesitant notes were struck. Ghastly, but workable. We went to get the permission of our still fuming landlord to play the instrument in the shed. By this time, the poor man thought we were crazy anyway, so he gave us the necessary blessing.

Now Mel's imagination took wing. "Let's not play for the spiders in this shed," he said. "Let's move the piano into my cabin!" I instantly recognized this as a first-rate idea and we started to move the instrument. Let's pause for a question. When was the last time you tried to move a piano some 100 yards through deep snow? If the answer is the expected "never," let me warn you to keep it that way. Mel and I were hopelessly out of shape anyway, and after tugging, pushing, and falling over for the tenth time, we saw that we had managed to move the antique box about five feet. It was like hauling Grant's Tomb through oatmeal. It was dark and cold but we were sweating with exertion.

Suddenly Mel had another brainstorm. "The hell with it; let's play right here, outside. We'll go back to the cabin and get two flashlights, bring them out here, and play al fresco." What could be more sensible? When Mel's wife Martha appeared from town an hour later, she came upon two grown men, bundled up to the eyes, playing four-hand Haydn symphonies in the lightly falling snow, two flashlights illuminating the scene. We never did quite comprehend why she got so excited.

Mel quit MGM soon after. He studied with Paul Hindemith, began to compose more and more, acquired a huge reputation among the avant garde, and wound up a professor at Yale. Currently he is the Dean of CalArts, a remarkable music school, and was 1990's Pulitzer winner. But I still remember his three choruses on "The World Is Waiting for the Sunrise," and I also know for a fact that he can play the piano while wearing mittens.

SEVEN

IT IS A MYSTERIOUS FACT—being a fine composer of popular songs does not necessarily mean having a thorough musical education, or even a modicum of technical prowess. Of course there have been wonderfully accomplished musicians who have written popular music: Kurt Weill, who used to love orchestrating his own shows, George Gershwin, Vernon Duke, Johnny Green, and quite a few others. But for every one of them, there are a dozen of the other kind, brilliantly gifted melodists to whom the technical aspects of composing are anathema. I'm not even glancing in the direction of most of today's rock musicians, to whom any instrument that does not plug into the wall is a museum piece, and to whom manuscript paper is as foreign a substance as rocket fuel would be to the rest of us. It always has been amazing that literally hundreds of achingly pretty songs have been danced to and wept over, and were created by composers who are afflicted with a kind of musical dyslexia. Many years ago, during one of the meetings of the music branch of the Academy of Motion Picture Arts and Sciences, a motion was proposed that anyone wishing to be eligible for an Academy Award in the music categories should be able to prove that he or she could actually read and write music. Not anything taxing, no composing of mirror fugues or analyzing the late Beethoven Quartets; just the writing down of the musical equivalent of "See Dick and Jane Go to the Store." It was a suggestion taken up with alacrity by a great many of the members of the music branch, myself included, until someone pointed out that, by that rule, Irving Berlin, for example, would be ineligible. It was a point that hit home.

Moss Hart used to tell the following story: When he was working on a Broadway musical called *Mr. President,* he was, quite rightfully, in awe of the show's composer, Irving Berlin, and could hardly wait for the day that Mr. Berlin would play through the new score for him. At last the momentous occasion came, and the creative forces of the play gathered in the Berlin sitting room, ready to be dazzled. Now it has to be admitted that Irving Berlin could only play the piano in one key, that even in that one key he was not exactly virtuosic, and that his rendering of songs was often chaotic. The recital began, and issuing from the piano and from the hands of the master came a succession of sounds that could only be described as hesitant, childish, and discordant. Moss grew more and more apprehensive and bewildered. When the demonstration had clanged to a halt, he had a stroke of brilliance. "Before I say anything, Irving," he said, "would you do me a great favor? Would you play 'Blue Skies' just once?"

The great songwriter must have been perplexed, but he complied and launched into "Blue Skies." The same discordant, hesitant, childish mess sounded forth. Moss was relieved. "It's a great score," he said happily. "Irving, you've done it again."

The point of this story, dredged from the apocrypha of theater legends, is that songwriters are a breed apart. Application of musical sophistication has very little to do with basic melodic genius. It isn't an inflammatory opinion to say that Irving Berlin's songs are better than Leonard Bernstein's, nor is the fact that Bernstein had more musical knowledge in his eyelashes than Berlin had in his whole persona up for debate. During my years at MGM, it was my good fortune to work for some of the most illustrious songwriters of our time. Their reactions to the work of arrangers and orchestrators varied wildly. Cole Porter was the most elegant of creatures, his manners as courtly as his dress. Only once did I hear him voice a vituperative opinion. I was working on the film version of *Kiss Me Kate,* and Cole had interpolated the song "From This Moment On" into the existing score, for use as an elaborate dance number. "I have to warn you about something before you start making this arrangement," he said to me, his voice quite angry. "This tune has been recorded by Woody Herman and his band. Have you ever heard of him?"

I nodded eagerly. "Well," he went on, "what they did to my tune is absolutely disgusting. It was turned into a loud, strident jazz mess, and the melody is just about unrecognizable. It's a good example of someone not having any idea what the tune is about!" He stopped, thought for a moment, and grew less choleric. Finally he smiled. "But what am I talking about. Your arrangements are always so theatrical and correct for the occasion, I'm sure I'll love what you write." And indeed, when he came to the recording, he was fulsome in his praise. "That's more like it," he said, smiling. "I knew you would understand the song."

I never told him that *I* had written the arrangement for Woody Herman as well.

Fritz Loewe was equally protective of his songs, but his view of the arranger's craft tended to be more Olympian. I first met him on *Gigi,* and I was a great fan of his Vienna-tinged, sentimental tunes. However, he tended to write rather thick piano accompaniments under the melodic line, which prompted me to ask whether he would mind if I made the orchestral versions a bit more transparent. This question was meant to be respectful and polite, since *all* piano parts have to be altered when orchestrated. Fritz's reaction was a bit unnerving. He drew himself up as far as his elevator shoes would allow, and his blue eyes were icy. For a moment I thought I was going to be the recipient of a Heidelberg sabre *Schmiss* across the cheek. "Tell me," he purred, "did you attend conservatory?" I bobbed my head in assent. "And when you were at conservatory, were you given piano pieces to orchestrate?" Again I agreed. "And when you did these assignments, did you elect to change Brahms?" There wasn't any answer then, and there isn't now.

WHEN I WAS STILL A TEENAGER and working for Johnny Green in any menial capacity offered, Jule Styne and Sammy Cahn were working on the score of an early Sinatra film. They were energetic and enthusiastic and Sammy has always been one of nature's funny men. Needless to say, they also wrote terrific tunes. One afternoon I was in Johnny's outer office, using a desk in order to do some really soul-searching work, such as writing an arrangement for Xavier

Cugat and debating whether I could leave instructions in the score for him to stuff his disgusting little Chihuahua dog into the tuba, when Jule came in. "Listen, kid," he said conspiratorially, "I've just written something I quite like, but I have a sinking feeling I've swiped the melody from somewhere. Lemme play it for you, see if you recognize it," and he went to the piano and played a pretty tune, *con amore*. It did indeed seem vaguely familiar, but I couldn't really place it. Besides, I was much too shy to accuse someone like Jule of plagiarism, even if it was unintentional. At this point, Sammy Cahn breezed in, exuding confidence and bonhomie. "Got something for me to work on, Jule?" he asked, sharpening a pencil. Jule repeated his little speech of doubt, and played the questionable melody again. Sammy frowned and thought. "Geez," he finally offered, "it does sound like something else, but I really like it. Let's work on it. Play it again."

Some fifteen minutes later, Sammy had half a lyric done, and the boys were markedly happier. Jule had just begun to play the tune again when Johnny Green walked in. Without breaking his stride, he asked, "What are you guys doing with the verse to 'Tea for Two'?"

Jule and Sammy looked at each other. There was quite a pause. Then, wordlessly, Jule tore up a sheet of paper and reached for a new one. By the way, the final result of their labors that week was called "Time after Time," one of their prettiest songs.

IRA GERSHWIN was so unfailingly kind-hearted and soft-spoken that his cronies dubbed him President of the Nice Guys Club. This was an unofficial club dedicated to the proposition that members were never allowed to speak disparagingly about a colleague's work. Any infraction of this rule meant being stricken from the ranks. As can be imagined, the membership, small to begin with, finally dwindled to two members, Ira, the president, and Leo Robin, the remaining member at large. Naturally, Leo wanted to be the sole survivor someday, so from time to time he would test Ira by inviting him to be critical and thereby abdicate his presidency. Months went by, to no avail, until one day, the following exchange took place. The two lyricists were in a car driving to Santa Barbara, and the radio was playing a cloying medley from the operetta *Sweethearts*. Leo carefully started a conversation by asking guilelessly, "Ira, do you think that every single note Victor Herbert ever wrote is first-rate?"

IRA (absentmindedly): "Well . . ."

LEO (triumphantly): "I got you, that's it, I'm the new president!!"

It was always a treat to visit Ira at home. He would sit peacefully and quietly, surrounded by marvelous paintings, and it was sometimes difficult to remember that he had been responsible for the most erudite, most romantic, and wittiest lyrics ever written. He, too, wanted his work to remain untampered with, but unlike most of his colleagues, he never voiced his objections in anger. One day, when I had gone to see him, he asked whether I would mind if he played a new record before we discussed *Porgy and Bess*. Ira had a standing order at the Beverly Hills Gramophone Shop to send him any new recordings of Gershwin songs, which resulted in small trucks unloading them every month. On this particular occasion, a new album by Frankie Laine had arrived, and Ira wanted to hear the singer's version of his standard " 'S Wonderful." He put the record on and stood about six feet from the speaker, which was built into the wall, flanked by Soutine and Toulouse-Lautrec. The band played a short introduction and the voice of Frankie Laine began to shout, "It's wonderful, it's marvelous . . ."

Ira took the cigar out of his mouth and spoke directly into the loudspeaker. "No, no," he said, "that's not right. If I had wanted to say 'It's wonderful,' I would have written 'It's wonderful.' I know the word 'it's.' What I wrote is ' 'S wonderful' and you are spoiling my song." Ira's voice was disappointed but calm. He put the cigar back into his mouth and listened to the rest of the record without moving. When it got to the coda, Mr. Laine repeated, "It's wonderful, it's marvelous," and Ira turned to me, looking sad and perplexed. "He's done it again," he said mournfully and turned the machine off.

When Ira's book *Lyrics on Several Occasions* was published, he wrote the story of being stuck for a rhyme after " 'bout five-foot-six or -seven," in the song "Looking for a Boy." The word "heaven" had already been used, and Ira discarded "seven" and "eleven," found that "Devon" was impractical, and "replevin" impossible. A copy of the book containing this story arrived at my house, and Ira had written the following on the frontispiece:

AN APOLOGY

How on earth in my rhyming of "heaven"
  Did Heaven not send me a sign
To feature the surname of talented Previn!
(Alas—for the note on p. 9!)

If ever this book has a 2nd edition—
  I vow, if alive at the time,
That "heaven" and "Previn" receive recognition
As the one unimpeachable rhyme.

With affection,
IRA.

ALAN JAY LERNER was an extraordinary man. His talent was legendary, his capacity for work amazing. He had bags of charm, and was a generous and kindhearted friend and colleague. His wit could be lethal.

My Fair Lady had a very long and difficult music schedule. One of the problems was that Audrey Hepburn could not do her own singing. She was certainly the most beautiful creature imaginable and a lovely actress, but her singing voice, especially when subjected to the mercilessly clear speakers of Cinemascope, was unacceptable. Since Rex Harrison was already firmly established as a master of *parlando,* a kind of half-spoken singing, the leading lady had to trill like a bird. Therefore, Marnie Nixon, a highly talented and experienced voice double, was hired and put to work. After many days of recording, she suddenly became rather difficult, and resisted Alan Jay Lerner's instructions. To be fair, he gave six directions per syllable, so her reticence was not entirely unwarranted. But on this particular day, she took off the earphones, bridling, and snapped, "Are you aware, Mr. Lerner, that I have dubbed the voice for Deborah Kerr and for Natalie Wood, and for dozens of others?"

Alan's reply was prompt and gentle. "And are you aware, dear, that all those ladies dubbed your face?"

Lerner was also wildly eccentric and opinionated. Once, when one of his many marriages was disintegrating, he offered me some advice. "Just remember," he lectured, "it's always the woman's fault. It doesn't matter what the argument is about or what the crisis is or what the bone of contention may be, if you just keep saying to yourself 'It's the woman's fault,' you'll be able to survive without too many scars." He nodded ernestly, satisfied that he had passed on a nugget of empirical knowledge.

Another time, during the period when he and I were writing the musical *Coco* for Katharine Hepburn, and when we worked together every single day for most of a year, I went to him, secure in his confidence and friendship. "Alan," I began rather ceremoniously, "I have a secret to tell you. It's something private and something that I can't divulge to anyone else, but I'd like your advice." Alan threw his hands up, rather like a soccer goalie warding off a good shot. "Hold it right there," he said quickly. "Don't tell me any secrets, I don't keep them. The minute you leave the house I'll be on the phone telling everyone. I love gossip, I have no scruples about it, I'll tell everybody, no secrets, I mean it!!" I was flabbergasted. I thought he was kidding. I reminded him that we were partners, working colleagues, we had known each other for years, if I couldn't trust him then who could I trust, and so on and on. Again he interrupted, and smiled his charming smile. "I'm serious," he insisted, "you mustn't ever tell me a secret, I won't keep it, not for five minutes." He meant it. I could see that he meant it. I didn't tell him.

Alan's reluctance to put the finishing touches on his lyrics was famous in the profession. He told me that during the writing of *My Fair Lady,* he had been stopped by the second line of the chorus of "I Could Have Danced All Night," and worked on it during a certain period of every day for weeks. He finally solved it by repeating the first line: "I could have danced all night, I could have danced all night!" Since the song is one of the best known in the American musical theater, it seems, with hindsight, that the line could never have been anything else, but Alan always preferred working his way through the Hampton Court maze to strolling down the straight path right next to it. He was a perfectionist and perhaps that was why he was so often unwilling to dot the final *i* or cross the final *t,* or perhaps he felt that while the song still had an unfinished line, it belonged only to him and wouldn't be sent out into the skeptical world. Whatever the reason, producers had been known to turn old and shaky waiting for that one undecided phrase, that one unrhymed line.

Alan brought me in to write four additional songs for the film *Paint Your Wagon* at Paramount Studios. He had an imposing set of offices on the second floor of the producers' building, with a view of a large, splashing fountain, and some dressing rooms formerly inhabited by Betty Hutton. We finished a song called "A Million Miles from Home," but as usual, there was one line missing in the lyric. My deal at the studio was complicated; I was being paid by the completed song, so until I actually handed in a finished copy to the music library, I didn't get paid. I cajoled and pleaded and conned and threatened Alan for several weeks, but that one line, the last line of the middle part of the song, still eluded him. On one particular day, it had grown late, it was past six, and everyone had gone home. Once again I asked Alan to finish the line. I explained my predicament. "Okay, kid, sure," he said, and reached for paper and pencil. Ten seconds later he glanced at his watch, murmured, "Oh God I forgot my dinner date, I'll finish this tomorrow," and started to tie his tie, put on his coat, pick up his briefcase, and run, all at the same time.

I don't quite know what possessed me, but something snapped. "Oh no," I snarled, and moved quickly to the door. The key was on our side of the door; I turned it, removed it from the lock, wheeled toward the window, and threw it out, where it landed, lucky bull's-eye, in the middle of the fountain. "Have you gone mad?" Alan wanted to know. He leapt to the phone, called the auto gate, and ordered them to find someone with a pass key to let him out. "That'll take quite a while," I said. "In the meantime, here's more paper and a pencil, *Finish the goddamned line!!!*" Alan began to laugh. He walked over to his stand-up desk. He always worked standing up, an eccentricity I envied because I loved the Dickensian clerk's desk he used. Within one minute he finished the line in question and gave it to me. I copied it into the music sheets, and when the studio handyman came to let us out, I went straight to the music library and handed the song in. At nine the next morning

I was paid. At ten, Alan changed his mind and took the line back. He never did alter it to anything he liked better.

Another manifestation of the same habit had occurred before, during the filming of *Gigi*. There was an unfinished line in one of the songs, and Alan refused to let anyone see the rest of the lyric before the final inspiration struck. Arthur Freed was the producer, and he had been a highly successful lyricist himself in bygone days. He did everything but offer Alan a new Rolls-Royce if he would show him the song. No dice. Finally, the calendar provoked the situation into something more serious. The song was due to be recorded and photographed, but Alan was steadfast in his refusal. Freed sent for me. He had an interesting request. "I'm going to give you a key to Alan's room at the George V," he said, lowering his voice. "I want you to use it while Alan is out, and steal the lyric from his desk and give it to me."

"Shall I get his cuff links and his watch while I'm at it?" I asked, but then I saw that he was serious. I suggested gently that he do his own breaking and entering, and Arthur, with a deep sigh, resigned himself to the situation. "Waltz at Maxim's" was recorded in Paris with six words missing, words that were inserted many weeks later, back in Hollywood.

One final reminiscence about Alan: I went one day to his house for an afternoon's work on *Coco,* and he opened the door, bubbling over with enthusiasm. He had a great idea, a *great* idea, he told me. His uncle was a renowned oceanographer, with a laboratory submarine. He suggested that he, Alan, and I could board and run this submarine and spend a couple of weeks on it. Feeling that I was standing very near the edge of a precipice, I asked why we should do this.

"I know where Atlantis is."

"What?"

"I know where Atlantis is," he repeated. "I've worked it out, and you and I will find it." He went into some detail. Atlantis, according to calculations, was on the bottom of the ocean, but at certain periods of time, it was high enough to be accessible, a bit like Debussy's "Cathedrale Engloutie." We would find it, he reasserted, and in the meantime, while we were looking for it, we could finish writing the show. On the submarine. By this time I knew Alan well enough to realize that he had to be dissuaded slowly and without impatience. I reminded him that in the annals of impractical men, he and I reigned supreme, that neither one of us could be trusted to change a light bulb, and that therefore running a two-man submarine was, let's say, foolhardy. He wasn't even stumped for a second. Okay, maybe I was right, in that case we would get a three-man sub and a fellow from the Navy to run it, this was a trifle, a mere *bagatelle* to throw in the way of such an achievement. Finally, I came up with a valid argument.

"Okay," I said, "okay. You and I get on the submarine, we work on the show, and we find Atlantis. We then steer the sub back to Florida, surface, and disembark. Then you say, 'Hi everybody, I'm Alan Lerner, I wrote *My Fair Lady,* and I've just found the lost continent of Atlantis in my submarine.' Alan, you're a playwright," I said. "Think of it as a scene in a play. Who's going to believe you? Who's going to think you're certifiable?"

The argument struck home. Alan was crestfallen. "Yeah, I guess you're right," he said sadly. He never brought the subject up again.

Like so many highly gifted men, Alan had a personality whirring with contradictions. At ease and full of charm in any company, he was also seething with nerves and anxieties. All his movements were quick and sudden, he walked at an extremely fast pace, and talked a mile a minute. He bit his fingernails so badly that he almost deformed his fingers. When the nails were gone, he would tear at the flesh of his fingertips, and at the cuticles. For a time, he thought that wearing short white cotton gloves, such as the ones film editors use when hanging on to film racing through the reels, would stop him, or at least slow him down. He wore them in venues of stress such as rehearsals of a play; the gloves would be on his hands, and then suddenly off, on again, ripped off again, plunged onto his hands again, over and over. As a final resort, he asked his secretary to always have a supply of lemon wedges at hand. He would take the lemon and massage and squeeze it over his raw fingers, never stopping his flow of directions and conversation, evidently hoping that the pain would prevent further biting. I watched him in the darkened Mark Hellinger Theatre, going through this ballet of gloves and lemons, and I was reminded of a scene in an ancient film called *The Lives of a Bengal Lancer,* in which the evil Khan jammed bamboo splinters under Gary Cooper's fingernails, and then set them on fire. I can only surmise that Alan had been as indelibly impressed by the viewing of that scene in his childhood as I had been in mine. My reaction was to avoid the scene at all costs, and Alan's had been to emulate it.

His pursuit of women was a lifetime calling, or obsession, or hobby, or whatever. But his lyrics were those of an incurable romantic; they are, for the most part, idealistic, the songs of a man continually falling in love. It is interesting to note that Cole Porter, whose involvement with ladies was a lot less vehement, wrote genuinely passionate songs. There are many references, oblique as well as direct, to carnal love, and the lyrics make many passes at physical intentions. Alan, whose life was a cauldron of entanglements, wrote about romance from a sweet and lofty plane.

MANY YEARS AGO, I was told the following story: Broadway producer Leland Hayward was about to put Maxwell Anderson's *Anne of the Thousand Days* onto the stage. He asked the author whom he envisaged as the ideal actor to portray Henry the Eighth. The playwright thought about it, then mentioned a good, safe, workmanlike actor of very little panache. "No, no," said Hayward. "Suppose there were absolutely no problems in getting anyone in the world you wanted—who would you name?"

Anderson immediately said, "Rex Harrison, but you'll never be able to get him."

Whereupon the producer grinned and said, "Why not ask him?" Then he made the necessary calls and, indeed, procured Rex Harrison's services.

"There's a lesson in this, Max," said the legendary Mr. Hayward. "Never start out asking for someone you would eventually settle for."

This sage piece of folklore came back to haunt me many years later. I was already living in London, and the suggestion had been made that I might like to write a stage musical based on J. B. Priestley's *The Good Companions*. Various lyric writers were suggested, all perfectly fine, none extraordinary. My undisputed idol among lyric writers was Johnny Mercer, whom I had only met once, fleetingly, at MGM, a dozen years previous. There was no earthly reason to suppose that he would contemplate a show with me, in London, after his staggering collaborations with the likes of Jerome Kern, Harold Arlen, and Harry Warren. But he was the best, and remembering the Maxwell Anderson story, I wrote Mercer a letter, trying not to get sickeningly sycophantic or flattering, but baldly asking would he like to write a show with me? The answer came back so promptly that I had visions of Johnny pacing up and down the street in front of his house, waiting for the mailman to bring him my suggestion.

"Yes," he said, and "what a fine idea," he said, and "I'll come over next month," he said.

Even before we actively began writing anything, we met regularly and often, talking and planning and generally having a very good time. Johnny told me that he wanted to see some new English musicals, to see what the London audience liked. The only one playing was an adaptation of a Pinero play, and we duly bought tickets and went. Halfway through act one I was abysmally bored, and by the time the intermission started, I was filled with rage and despair. "Let's get out of here," I said. "This is hopeless." Johnny looked at me mildly. "Now, now, old boy," he said, "you're being unkind and impatient. This is the very first show these two authors have written, their first time at bat, and it would be nice of you to be a bit more charitable."

I felt small and mean, and regretted my absence of human kindness. To cover my embarrassment I leafed through the program. "Wait a minute," I stage-whispered. "Look at the authors' biographical sketches. This isn't their first show, it's their fourth!"

Johnny's expression never changed. "Their fourth?" he asked. I nodded. "Let's go," he said and was out in the aisle before I could even grab my coat.

He used to come over to my house in Surrey, open his briefcase, and sit down near the big fireplace. Somehow, being surrounded by English country antiques, old pub signs, and floribunda roses swaying against leaded windows made him seem even more Southern. No matter how urban and sophisticated Johnny became throughout his life, he was never far away from Savannah, Georgia. He brought wonderful presents: buckets full of Southern pecans, and for my daughter Lark's birthday, he wrote a special lyric to his song

"Skylark." Our work habits were complementary. Johnny worked very quickly; so did I. On those occasions when I wrote the melody first, he would sit and stare at the paper and then be able to write a wonderful first-draft lyric without having to hear the tune over and over again. By the same token, if the words came first, I would sit in silence, manuscript paper on my lap, and write the tune without trying it on the piano first.

He told me a lovely story about his craft. A lady stopped him and told him that she, too, was a lyricist. As a fellow writer, she confided, she was interested in knowing the step-by-step procedure he used in approaching a new song. Johnny obliged. "I examine the reason for the song, the exact situation in which it is to be sung, and I'm careful about exactly who is to sing it. Then I try to get a title phrase, a memorable phrase which would occur either at the beginning or the end of the structure. Then, once I've got that far, I get out my rhyming dictionary and—" The woman interrupted him by making disapproving, clucking sounds. "You use a rhyming dictionary?" she asked, in a voice as patronizing as Margaret Thatcher's. Johnny was bewildered. "Yes, of course." "Oh well, in that case, no wonder," she told him, and left.

John loved that story, and would roar with laughter when he told it. He fell in love with the names of English villages. As a lyricist, he adored them, and I made him happy by giving him a gazeteer of the British Isles. "Listen to this," he would say, leaf through the pages, and recite: "Lower Beeding, Much Birch, Clayton-le-Woods, Bodymoor Heath, Copdock, Middle Wallop, Bishops Tawton, Climping, and Barnham Broom. Isn't that great?" Finally, we wrote a song for the play in which a troup of actors are trying to find out where to change trains in order to get to innumerable places the names of which Johnny couldn't resist. Its appeal may have been a bit limited, but we both loved it.

I was very happy during the time we worked together. John's lyrics are inimitable. He has a particular blend of the deeply poetic and sweetly vernacular that no other lyricist has been able to approach. He was a lovely human being, helpful to me, avuncular to my children, productive, inventive, and a joy to be with. He wore his fame lightly, and with grace. His scorn was reserved for the frauds and for the pretenders in the business, and he had no time at all for the emperor's new clothes.

Our show opened to what is euphemistically called "mixed reviews." It was by no means a smash. My favorite memory is the making of the demonstration records—Johnny singing and myself accompanying. He was a dynamite singer: Southern to the core, blessed with the immaculate time-keeping of a jazz instrumentalist, and able to imbue any given 32-bar phrase with humor and feeling. If he had never written a word, he would still have been my favorite singer.

I WOULD BE REMISS if I didn't touch briefly on the surprising lyric-writing efforts of Kim Novak. I was working for Billy Wilder on his film *Kiss Me, Stupid,* and I had been asked to teach Miss Novak the melody of a song she had to sing a few days hence. I met with Miss Novak, who turned out to be not only beautiful and charming, but quick to learn the tune in question. As we were preparing to leave the sound stage at Goldwyn Studios, where a piano had been brought in for the afternoon, she asked me whether I was familiar with the theme, by Franz Waxman, from "A Place in the Sun." Yes, I told her, I did know it, and thought it quite beautiful.

"Oh, so do I," she said, "and I wrote a lyric for it, even though no one asked me to." I was intrigued. "What do you call the song?" I asked.

"To Be or Not to Be," she told me earnestly.

There was a little silence. "Interesting idea," I managed. "How does it go?"

She was very surprised. "Don't you know it?" she demanded.

"Oh, yes, sure I know it," I said, "I just had never thought of it as a pop song before. How does the lyric go on?"

"I thought you'd know," she said, with just a touch of condescension. "It goes on, 'That is the question.'"

"Ah yes, fine, certainly," I tried to regain ground, "and what happens after that?"

"After that," she said, and smiled a smile of great sweetness, "after that it's original."

EIGHT

TOWARD MOVIE ACTORS, whose self-absorption tends to be on the same level as that of operatic tenors, my fondness is less broad. But one whose memory still gives me pleasure is Louis Calhern. Tall, distinguished-looking and well-spoken, he had played Lear and Oliver Wendell Holmes, and he invariably gave the appearance of someone very high up in the Foreign Office. In fact, he was raffish and funny. Once I passed him on the street when he was in full costume as a sort of Ruritanian general. His uniform was sky blue and he was festooned with medals. I pointed to the most garish of these and asked him what it had been awarded to him for. "For having been married to Ilka Chase," he explained.

When I was conducting the score to an unbelievably bad epic called *The Prodigal,* he came to the recording stage, diffidently made his way to the podium, and asked whether I minded his staying and watching. I told him I was pleased that he was interested and invited him to stay as long as he wished. Instantly his manner changed and he became his elegant, cigarette-holder self again. He turned and said loudly, "Someone cause a chair to be placed here for me!!" and waited imperturbably for this to be carried out. He also chided me for making a date with a dancer. "Take my advice," he counseled kindly, "forget it with chorus girls. Find somebody older. Get some cuff links."

I had watched the unspooling of *The Prodigal* and was mystified by some of the ramifications of the plot. Calhern played a kind of pagan temple priest in it.

"Lou," I asked, "why did you have Lana Turner thrown into the flames as a sacrifice?" Calhern thought only for a moment.

"Pique," he said.

ANN MILLER was a superb dancer. She was also good-natured and hard-working and devoid of "star" mannerisms. Of course it has to be admitted that Ann was untroubled by the teachings of Stanislavsky, and undisturbed by the maxims of Coquelin. Her horizons were firmly fixed to the landscape of musical comedy. When the road company of *Death of a Salesman* reached Los Angeles, she stopped by a table in the MGM café to ask what the play was about, and would she enjoy it. The cast at the table included Hermes Pan, the choreographer, Norman Corwin, the writer, Stanley Donen, the director, and me. We were baffled by the question; *Salesman* had been the most discussed play in many a season, everyone knew of its power, and none of us were able to give a concise answer. Finally Norman tried. "It's about failure, and about the American Dream," he said. "It's about a man's love for his sons, and about his ultimate demise." Annie giggled happily. "Whooey," she tinkled, "not my thing, guess I'll skip it," and off she went.

I happened to be on the set when she was filming a scene in a taxi. The taxi was in front of a process screen and appeared to be careening madly down the street, with another car in hot pursuit. The other actors in the cab were reacting wildly to their plight, trying to keep their balance, and looking apprehensively behind them. Ann sat primly and recited her lines as if she were sitting in a warm bath. The director stopped the proceedings and spoke to her in tones of controlled impatience. "Are you aware, darling," he asked, "that the car behind you is trying to overtake you, that it is full of gangsters, and that they will try to shoot you and maybe kill you? And that perhaps you shouldn't be quite so calm about it?"

Annie was unperturbed. What was this man getting at? Why was he upset? "Of course I'm aware of it, honey," she reassured him. "Relax! I'm just not acting yet."

But boy! She could certainly tap dance!

DURING THE YEARS I lived in Los Angeles I saw quite a lot of Jack Lemmon. I met him through Billy Wilder and instantly liked him.

Jack is smart and funny and unpretentious. He is also a pretty good pianist, adores music, and writes nice songs. He has an offbeat sense of the descriptive, and his conversation sometimes takes unexpected twists and turns. One afternoon during the time we were both working on *Irma la Douce,* he was sitting in the garden of my house when I asked him whether he had met the new husband of a friend of ours. She was a superior lady and we were all very fond of her. "Yeah, I've met him," said Jack slowly. There was a kind of Pinterian pause. I pressed forward. "What's he like, is he nice?" Jack took his time answering. "Look at it this way," he finally offered. "Here I am sitting in your house, and I'm wearing a red baseball cap. Now, it's all right with you that I'm wearing a red baseball cap, isn't it, I mean, you wouldn't even take notice of it, right?"

I was mystified but agreed that I wouldn't take notice of it or find fault with it. Jack went on. "And if you came to my house wearing a red baseball cap, it would be perfectly okay and I wouldn't even mention it, right?"

Again I agreed that this would be the case. Jack drove home his point and his voice quickened. "Well," he said, "if her new husband walked in now, and he were wearing a red baseball cap, both you and I would take one look and say, 'Who's the schmuck in the red hat?' " And he leaned back, satisfied that his character analysis had been precise and complete, which of course it had been.

REX HARRISON was quite a different breed from Jack, and that is understatement run amok. His outward self-assurance was only a cover-up for an even greater self-assurance underneath, and there seemed to be only two ways to approach any problem: his way and the wrong way. He left quite a few battered egos on the road, but when the final result was the kind of incandescent comedy acting of which he was the master, there were few lasting quibbles.

When Rex heard that I had been engaged by Warners to serve as musical director for the film version of *My Fair Lady,* he flew into a rage. "I won't have it, I don't want him," he hissed at Alan Lerner. "For the entire run of the play, both on Broadway and in London, we had Franz Allers conducting the orchestra. Franz knows exactly how I sing and how I speak, my cadences and my rhythms. There's no one like Franz, that's who I want, that's who we must get." Alan

The scoreboard hanging over the orchestra made life for the local critics much easier.

In those days, the London Symphony Orchestra was not used to conductors in T-shirts.

With Vladimir Ashkenazy at a rehearsal in the early sixties. Both of us still had black hair.

I appear to be controlling traffic, the violinists aren't playing, and Vladimir Ashkenazy is checking his hairline—where was the music?

Ah, the sixties! Look at those trousers! I had no shame.

This time the prize was for *Irma la Douce*. I'm standing with Sammy Davis and Elmer Bernstein.

My teacher, Pierre Monteux, was deeply happy when he was made an honorary fireman. Can you guess which one is Le Maître?

This apprehensive-looking quartet consisted of myself, J. B. Priestley, Ronald Harwood, and Johnny Mercer. We were working on a musical.

With Debbie Reynolds and the Sherman brothers. Shortly after winning this Oscar for *My Fair Lady,* I left Hollywood.

My old friend Shelly Manne, who kept time for everybody and
never had an unkind word to say.

I was sent this photo by a fan. It is without doubt my favorite picture, since it proves how attentive my audiences are.

tried: "André conducts great orchestras in difficult repertoire, he'll be just fine for you," but Rex was off and running, extolling the unique virtues of Franz Allers and reminding Alan that conducting a symphony orchestra had nothing to do with following and accompanying his, Rex's, style of presenting a number.

I had no quarrel with his opinion of Franz Allers, a distinguished colleague, but I had already been assigned to the film. Then Alan had a fine idea. He persuaded Rex to try—"just try"—recording a number with me. Then, when it didn't work out, Rex could go to Jack Warner and have me replaced with Franz, without ever seeming to be arbitrary or demanding. Rex saw the wisdom of such a subterfuge, and we scheduled the recording of "Let a Woman in Your Life." It went perfectly smoothly, Rex had no problems, the orchestra and I had no problems, and the song was finished ahead of schedule. That night, Alan called Rex from New York: "How did it go? Was it difficult? Did you get any of it finished?" Rex interrupted him, "Yes, yes, dear boy," he shouted, "it was terrific. I get along fine with André, and he followed my singing without the slightest trouble. In fact, he was certainly better than that Germanic son of a bitch we used to have in the pit!"

CERTAINLY the most interesting men I met in Hollywood were the directors.

There is no doubt in my mind that the film maker I most admired in Hollywood was Billy Wilder. I had the good fortune to compose four scores for him: *Irma la Douce, Fortune Cookie, One Two Three,* and *Kiss Me, Stupid.* He was a far cry from the imperious producers who asked their composers to audition their "themes" for them before they were recorded, and who then demanded countless changes and rewrites, all stemming from an ignorance of music only outdone by an unending need to flaunt authority. Not so with Billy. He would run the film for me and then discuss it at length, but always in dramatic terms, not in specific musical demands. These suggestions of Billy's were unfailingly correct.

I remember a long scene in *Irma la Douce* in which Jack Lemmon, the complete innocent, prepared for his first carnal night with Shirley MacLaine. The sequence was full of jokes, both verbal and visual, and the trap of underlining all the comedic bits with music was certainly seductive. Billy asked me to write romantic music instead; not erotically romantic, but sweetly and simply so, disregarding all the pratfalls. Of course he was right, and the final result was curiously touching.

Once Billy had had these discussions with me—or, I presume, with any of his film's composers—he would leave me totally alone to get on with it. If the film had lots of music in it, I might take six weeks to write it; less if the demands of the music were not too stringent.

I would not see Billy again until the first day of recording with the orchestra. Then he would appear, remain in the back of the sound stage, and wander around, back and forth, twirling one of his ever-present caps in his hand. No comments were forthcoming from him. I guess he figured that if the score was bad, he was under no obligation to use it or to hire me again, but in the meantime, professional courtesy precluded his interfering with what had obviously been the end result of a great deal of thinking on my part.

I was fascinated by his private musical preferences. He, the renowned cynic, the acknowledged master of the destructive quip, had a sentimental streak a mile wide when it came to music. One time, in his apartment, he stood by the record player, entranced and happy, listening over and over to a neglected and unknown waltz by Josef Strauss, on an ancient record conducted by Hans Knappertsbusch. He sang along with the orchestra, oblivious and vulnerable, and only when it was over did he remember to make the expected acerbic remark.

Billy had one of the most renowned painting collections in America. He had run out of wall space years earlier, but that never stopped him from acquiring yet another object of his admiration. In a city where the selection of great paintings was often left to the advice of a financial manager, Billy's collection was personal and beautiful. One of his passions was the work of Egon Schiele, and he managed to acquire quite a number of the tortured Viennese canvases. One time, we were leaving the studio at the same time, and Billy invited me up to his place. "I have something new and beautiful to show you." Once we arrived in his living room, he went to a closet and brought out his new Schiele watercolor. It was one of the master's more luridly explicit efforts: an emaciated young woman, green-tinged flesh, sunken cheeks, hopeless eyes, naked, and about to engage in what used to be called self-abuse. Billy contemplated the picture with total concentration. "Isn't it great?" he said.

At this moment, his wife Audrey came in the front door. Audrey is chic and dear and extremely funny. As she passed us, she gave a quick glance of horrified appraisal.

"Good God, Billy," she said. "Just once! Buy a landscape!"

Most of *One Two Three* was shot in Munich. A lot of the dialogue consisted of extremely barbed comments on the German psyche, since Billy, like most of his generation, had deep and permanent feelings about the more Teutonic aspects of Deutschland. He was interviewed by a young German newspaperman, whose blond crew-cut and military bearing didn't do much to endear him to Billy. In an accent which would have made Otto Preminger sound like Gielgud, the reporter asked, "Mr. Wilder, you lived here when you were a young man; how would you sum up your feelings on this, your first return in decades?"

Billy leaned back in his chair and began to answer in an affable, almost avuncular tone of voice, a clear danger signal to those who knew him well.

"When I lived here as a very young man, I was dead broke. No money at all, and few prospects. I had a tiny room in a sort of garret. The walls were paper thin, and on the other side of the wall nearest my bed was a toilet. The toilet was broken and flushed all night long. I used to pretend to myself that it was the sound of the river, which ran past the hotel. Now, as you say many decades later, I'm back. I have lots of money and I am very successful. I have this spacious suite in the hotel and a balcony which affords me a great view. Once again, the river is nearby, and at night, with the balcony doors open, I can hear the hypnotic movement of the water. But it keeps me awake, and do you know why? Because all I can think of is that goddamned toilet!"

ANOTHER WONDERFUL DIRECTOR who was inimitable, and great fun to work with, was Norman Jewison. Actually, I met him long after I had given up Hollywood. I was already living in England and was the principal conductor of the London Symphony Orchestra. Norman called when he was having mountains of problems getting the score of *Jesus Christ Superstar* recorded. I wasn't too frantically busy at the time, and I had always admired Norman's films, so I was pleased to accept the assignment. The film had wall-to-wall music and it turned out to be a wildly complicated business, since much of it had been shot with only a so-called guide track of drums and rhythm, and reams of orchestral music were missing. To be frank, I loathed the music but admired Norman's solution of how to put the show on film.

Norman is an immensely entertaining man. He is small and agile, and his enthusiasms are catching. He is a brilliant raconteur. If there is such a thing as a Canadian leprechaun, he would qualify for the part. He is also good-natured and patient. I only saw him vent to exasperation once during *Jesus Christ Superstar*. I was in a projection room together with the music editor Dick Carruth and I was dictating instructions when Norman happened to walk in.

"We need music as soon as the song proper is finished," I said. "Let's start on the big close-up of the kid in the white suit."

Norman gave an anguished wail. "What kid in the white suit," he demanded. "Can't you refer to him as Jesus?"

"No, Norman," I said callously, "not after that song he just finished!"

For the recording sessions, I had managed to put together a very starry orchestra of some eighty-five musicians. In London it is always simple to procure the services of the best of the symphony orchestra musicians, if they are not actually in the middle of a concert. English musicians are so lamentably, shockingly underpaid that they will happily grasp at any outside extra employment. I've seen members of the London Symphony, the Royal Philharmonic, and the Covent Garden Orchestra, all sitting in a semicatatonic state, accompanying Cliff Richards during a recording date. At these recording sessions, it is a peculiarity of the English system that the musicians are paid off in cash at the end of each date. They queue up and get their pay packet, somewhat like up-market factory workers. One of the sessions on *Superstar* ended, and I was chatting to Norman, when the renowned Horn virtuoso Alan Civil, whose recordings of the Mozart Horn Concertos had traveled around the world, came up to me, stuffing his earnings into his pocket. "Hello, André," he said, "why are you conducting this piece of shit?"

"Hello, Alan," I answered. "May I introduce you to Mr. Norman Jewison, who produced and directed the film!"

Alan was unfazed. Not for nothing had he spent years sitting in an orchestra and coping with Karajan and Klemperer. He was instantly enthusiastic and fulsome. "I'm really happy to meet you," he said, "I've always loved your film *The Cincinnati Kid.*" I doubt whether Prince Metternich ever turned a moment more deftly.

Some weeks after the film was finished, Norman came to a concert of mine at the Royal Festival Hall. I was conducting the London Symphony, and the major work of the evening was Beethoven's Ninth. Unless insane mishaps occur during the performance, this particular monumental work always elicits great huzzahs at the end, and this occasion was no exception. There was a huge and enthusiastic reception, and I went to my dressing room extremely happy.

The next day Norman rang me, chortling and giggling on the phone. He had taken along as his guest a very well-known Hollywood film composer, a fine musician but one whose horizons had never encompassed any music other than the kind that has to be played while wearing headphones. The two gentlemen headed for a late dinner after the concert, and over coffee, Norman allowed himself a generous, if slightly sentimental, pronouncement. "It's nice, isn't it, to see André here in London, at the Festival Hall, with his own orchestra, getting cheered because of his performance of Beethoven's Ninth."

His friend nodded. "Sure, Norman," he said, "but you have to admit it's a shame how completely he screwed up his career!"

THE MOST RENOWNED pacifier of difficult ladies was the director of *My Fair Lady,* George Cukor. One of the most famous film directors ever, he was urbane and witty, a wonderful host, a good friend, and a perfectionist dynamo on the set. I was immensely fond of him and admired his work deeply. Part of his fame rested with the fact that he had always been able to calm the most excitable of the willful leading ladies of the 1930s, and had got some of their best performances from them. While George was in the Army during the war, he was assigned to the Signal Corps Movie Unit, which was run by Frank Capra. One day he was called to Capra's office on Long Island.

"Get a cameraman and an editor, and go to the Pentagon. General Patton is back from Europe and he'd like to make a filmed statement in his office." George duly took off for Washington, D.C., with two cohorts. At the Pentagon they were told to set up the camera and the lights in the general's office and wait for his imminent return. Cukor took a disbelieving look around the stark quarters.

"Good Lord," he said, his sophisticated taste affronted, "crossed swords behind the desk! How on the nose can we get? Let's take them down, move the desk in front of the window, and see if we can get a better chair." His two co-workers were apprehensive. Patton was a man who wore a steel helmet at all times, carried a revolver, and was not given to a lot of patience. But George was not to be swayed; after all, he was back in his element, he was directing film, and the fact that he was a buck private about to deal with the scourge of Rommel did not enter his mind. The swords were taken down and the desk was in mid-move when Patton flung open the door and walked in. His rage was instant and fearful. He screamed at the top of his voice, "What do you think you're doing, you unspeakable Hollywood bastards!" This was only the beginning of a flow of invective of which Blackbeard the Pirate would have been proud. George sighed deeply with resignation. He was not at all frightened. Joan Crawford, Norma Shearer, Greta Garbo—he had dealt with tantrums all his life. He walked over to the general, who was now nearing the fortissimo apex of his wrath, and put his arm around the shoulder with the four stars on it. "Now, General," he said, soft-voiced and persuasive, "are we going to be silly about this?"

The cameraman and the editor blanched. Visions of firing squads or guillotines danced in front of them. Patton stopped in mid-threat. Never had he heard a sentence remotely like the one this private had just uttered. The insanity of the moment got to him, and he laughed and laughed. The swords were put back, the newsreel was filmed, and George Cukor went back to the Signal Corps base, innocent of the dire consequences his friends had deemed inevitable.

VERY OFTEN, when thinking or talking about my film days, in order to remind myself forcibly of how long ago it all was, I will organize those events as having happened in "my other life." It is a self-indulgence, but like many convenient excuses, there is a lot of truth in the phrase. How could it have been anything but another life, when it involved so little that is pertinent to my existence today? Different ambitions, different plans, methods of work I can no longer identify with, triumphs and disappointments that would not cause a twitch on the Richter scale that governs my life today.

Luckily there is one aspect of those years that is as important to me now as it was then: I made a lot of friends then whose friendship is as vital this week as it was twenty-five years ago. In a Utopian world, this would be taken for granted, and for all I know, in professions governed by school loyalties and country clubs, it is the norm, but in the world of professional performers it can't be relied upon. I don't think this has to do with the natural flightiness of the entertainment industry and the performing arts, but rather with the circumstances governing them.

IN THE FILM WORLD, each movie throws together a number of volatile people—working together, eating together, sharing the same schedule, gossiping, relaxing, and reacting to more or less the same problems for a number of highly concentrated weeks or months. Then, suddenly, it is completely over and done. Everyone disperses to new assignments, different studios, and periods of waiting which are usually both anxious and lonely, until the next onslaught of hyperactivity, more than likely with totally different people. No wonder friendships are made quickly and neglected quickly; continuity is rare. Obviously this is not as true for those of us working behind the camera as it is for those wearing makeup. Back in my day, the big studios had writers, directors, cameramen, and composers under contract; we were supposed to help fashion the style of the particular lot we worked on, and we were, by comparison, stable.

I met Blake Edwards shortly after I went to work at MGM. Blake has long been established and distinguished, but when I first ran into him in 1950, he was still writing radio dramas and barely getting a foothold in the studios. Everyone recognized him as a young man full of talent and promise, and he was personable and funny. We were both bachelors, and occasionally would run into one another at restaurants with our girls in tow.

Sometime around then I was focusing my attention on a wonderfully pretty young actress, who paid me the sweet compliment of giving me a gold key to her apartment, a conceit I thought had gone out with the *Ziegfeld Follies*. That key meant a lot to me: It made me feel racy and raffish, and I loved using it. One evening I left the lady's flat and went whistling down the flight of stairs leading to the street. Halfway down, there was Blake, on his way up. We waved, "Hi, Blake," "Hi, André," and as we passed on the steps, we each saw a glint of light, a small flash, in the other's hand. We stopped and looked at each other. I was in the act of putting my key away, Blake was just getting his out. We compared our tokens of fidelity. No doubt about it, we were keeping company with a generous girl. We were both very young and it wasn't important. We descended to the street together and went to have dinner. Each of us kept affectionate thoughts about the lady in question, despite the disillusionment about exclusivity.

Blake's films have made me laugh uncontrollably over the years, especially the wildly physical bits. Sight gags tend to pale on the printed page, but I have my favorites: The dapper hero alights from a taxi at the airport and steps into a storm of tornado force. He opens his umbrella—in the direction the gale is blowing, naturally —and is literally whipped out of the scene, catapulted out of view as if snapped away by a giant rubber band. In another film, a private detective hides in a bathroom closet, with only his one hand visible on the outside door frame. Leading lady enters and, without looking, slams the closet door shut. Nothing stirs, not a sound is made. Only after the heroine leaves the room is there a ghastly groan from inside the cupboard. Blake also loves the innocent bystander, bewildered by the mayhem exploding around him. A man tries to cross the street in a normally deserted village, and is stopped by a sudden onslaught of roaring traffic. The traffic disappears, the man tries again. Another wave of screaming tires and smoking exhaust. The man jumps back on the curb in alarm. He tries twice more, with the same result. Finally, although now the village is serene again, the man has been permanently cowed, gives up, and disappears back into the house whence he came. Unlike Billy Wilder, whose jokes are verbal and complicated, Blake has a sense of humor that can be traced back to happier, naiver times. He is not known to shy away from pie throwing, and you can bet that if there is a ditch in the street, someone will fall into it. I'm sure Blake operates on the theory that if something strikes him as funny, he puts it into his films. If he himself is not amused, the gag will be passed over. I, for one, am a permanent patsy for his brand of humor, and the more outrageous his images become, the more I will laugh.

Blake is married to Julie Andrews, whom I met well before every child in the civilized world could ask whether she could really fly around a room. Julie, despite her sweetness, has obviously made a pact with the devil, since the passing years choose not to leave a mark on her. She is also a deeply nice woman. "Nice," in today's usage, is almost pejorative, interchangeable with "square," and redolent of Louisa May Alcott. In Julie's case, nice also means friendly, delightful, pleasing, and congenial. What it does not encompass is the other side of her personality, which is raucous and ribald and hip. For quite a while she drove around town with a bumper sticker that read MARY POPPINS IS A JUNKIE, and it is a pleasure to hear her produce a loud dirty laugh. Most English women look great carrying a garden basket over one arm, but their sense of humor is a holdover from Elizabethan days. I'm convinced of it. I ought to know, I'm married to one of them.

IT WAS MIKE NICHOLS who introduced me to Julie all those years ago. I met Mike while I was toiling at Warner Brothers and Mike was launching his production of *Who's Afraid of Virginia Woolf?* with Elizabeth and Richard Burton. I visited his set often, and he came around to the recording stage. We liked each other's company; we tended to laugh at the same things and admire the same people. At the time, he was renting a large house that had once belonged to Cole Porter. I did not think the house looked like Cole Porter, nor did it have much to do with Mike. It was just one of those large California houses with a pool and a lot of alarmingly white furniture.

Mike would fill the house with friends, usually displaced New York friends, and we would start endless, driven rounds of word games. "Dictionary" was an early favorite, a game in which the correct definition of an arcane word was copied out of the Oxford Dictionary. Then each participant would be asked to write down a fabricated definition. All the definitions would be read aloud, and everyone cast votes as to the correct one. I still remember that Mike blew an entire round one night by being totally unable to read with a straight face that the meaning of the given word was "any statue of a chicken." He was weeping with laughter, and the fact that this definition turned out to be the true one did not help.

The damndest people casually wandered in and out of that house, ready for games: Jerome Robbins, Steve Sondheim, Anthony Perkins, Bob Carrington, George Segal, Robert Redford, and Lillian Hellman. It is barely possible that Mike is not acquainted with the head traffic warden in Peekskill, but other than that, I have a feeling he knows everybody.

Gradually we found out facts about each other that were fairly startling. He was born in Berlin. I was born in Berlin. We were close to the same age, his father (a doctor) and my father (a lawyer) both took their families out of Germany and to Paris at the last minute, toward the end of 1938. Mike and his family, and I and mine, came over on the same ship, the *S.S. Manhattan.* The first film we each saw was *Test Pilot,* with Clark Gable, and the first time we went to the theater, it was to see *Arsenic and Old Lace.* As these various disclosures surfaced, they became a bit spooky to us. A few years later, I was walking around Beverly Hills with my mother when we ran into Mike. I introduced them and they chatted for a while. When she subsequently turned to walk into a shop, Mike grabbed my arm. "You have my mother," he said, just a bit pale.

When a German child attends his very first day of school, it is a custom to give him a *"Tüte"* to take along. A *Tüte* is a large cone-shaped container, and it is filled with sweets and cookies and delicacies for the kid—a kind of protection against the possible cruelties of a first encounter with reality. When Mike headed for his first day of shooting *Who's Afraid of Virginia Woolf?* I found an old-time director's megaphone, which is exactly the correct shape of the school *Tüte*. I had his name painted along the side in German script, and I filled it with salami, Black Forest ham, pumpernickel, and other Kraut remembrances. It was delivered to him as he left his house on that first morning, and needed no explanation. He remembered perfectly. Our formative years had enough parallels to make us sympathetic to the other's feelings and reactions. Although we did not spend our childhood years together, we had the same childhood. It is a permanent, if subconscious, link. One of the few disciplines we did not share was my passion for jazz. And yet, Mike shares an attitude with the jazz players: that of being able to pick up a relationship after years of absence, and to pick it up without drama or fuss.

Nowadays I see him in New York; in Connecticut, where he raises horses, or in London, where we again seem to have many of the same friends. In all the years of our friendship, I have never worked with him. I conduct a lot in Vienna; I wish he would direct a production of *Der Rosenkavalier* at the opera there, and I could conduct. Instead of the presentation of the Silver Rose, perhaps on that evening it could be a silver statue of a chicken.

THERE'S A GREAT DEAL GOING ON behind the scenes of a film that is unsung and unpublicized.

Not long ago, my wife Heather and I were watching *Easter Parade* on television, mesmerized, as usual, by Fred Astaire's sleight-of-feet. As his dance routines grew more and more complex, Heather gave a low whistle of admiration. "I just don't understand how he could keep his taps so rhythmic, so flawless, so clean, on take after take," she said. "Listen to him, it's like a perfect drum pattern. Perfect every time."

I agreed that there was no one like him. "However," I said, in on the secrets of moviemaking, "the taps are put in later, long after the photography is finished."

My darling helpmate looked at me with a certain revulsion. "That's not true," she said. "How can you fabricate such a petty lie?"

I laughed and tried to sound off-hand. "Don't be silly, darling, it's true all right, but the taps are recorded and put onto the film much later, usually by the dancer himself but sometimes by dance assistants who have been known to put tap shoes on their hands in order to keep the patterns sounding perfect."

"Oh really?" she said, scorn dripping from her pretty lips. "And are the dancers' foot movements drawn in later by cartoonists and their voices dubbed by ventriloquists?"

Well, I tried explaining. I tried delineating the process of recording the music first, photographing the action afterward, but keeping the process of photography silent so that a new and immaculate sound track could be substituted later. This, I said triumphantly, necessitated the dance being shot silently, and the taps being put in later. "When a number doesn't quite work," I said, "the phrase 'It'll be fine once we get the taps in' is quite commonplace during the making of a musical."

My wife stood and drew herself imperiously to her full height. She is taller than I am, I must tell you at this point, so it is a very fine maneuver. "Absolute rubbish," she said in withering British accents, and left the room to pore over her Fred Astaire scrapbooks.

I brought the subject up once more, the next day. Heather, rather unkindly I thought, brought up the fact that I had once told her that I must be the only living musician, supposedly talented, who had not been able to learn the basic time-step from either Fred Astaire or Gene Kelly. Both these kindly Titans had wasted some valuable time in rehearsal halls, attempting to show me this step, which is taught to three-year-old kiddies in patent leather shoes within five minutes. At first they thought my clumsiness hilarious, then pitiful, then inexplicable, and finally enraging. "My God," snarled Fred, walking in little circles and kicking at the floor with suede shoes, "I had to teach this step to a bear in the circus once, and he caught on pretty smartly—what's the matter with you?"

It was my wife's theory that I, still smarting under the memory of my shameful lack of coordination, had made up the farfetched theory of postsynchronizing taps. Nevertheless, it does happen to be true. It is also true that the music film editors often were called upon to deliver really heroic efforts. In the 1940s and early 1950s, MGM was inordinately fond of musical films involving operatic singing. Jeanette MacDonald and Nelson Eddy had set the trend in the thirties, and the studio badly wanted to groom stars who could take their place, an ambition truly worthy of the more bizarre flights of the Grand Guignol. Kathryn Grayson was one singing lady deemed worthy of the MacDonald mantle, and she trilled her way through many a Technicolor epic. She was perfectly nice and could get around tunes by Jule Styne or Jerome Kern, but realizing that immortality lay in sterner scores, she would announce periodically that she was planning to accept an invitation from the Metropolitan the following year. She probably confused the Metropolitan Insurance Company with the opera house in New York, because the Met, callous as they are, never took her up on the idea. So here she was, limiting her output to the film studio where, I remember, she essayed the Bell Song from *Lakmé* in a Frank Sinatra–Jimmy Durante movie called *It Happened in Brooklyn.* The Bell Song is not easy; it spends a lot of time in the stratospheric heights of coloratura *tessitura,* and it was all a bit much for our heroine. What is heard on the finished sound track is the result of over 150 edited intercuts, meaning that almost every squeak is from a different take.

Then there is the time-honored system of dubbing voices onto nonsinging actors. That's a fairly simple process: If a leading actor or actress is called upon to sing on the screen but can at best make a tiny croaking sound, then a professional singer is brought in and recorded. The record is then given to the actor, who practices moving his lips, mouth, and throat to the sound track, and who is ultimately photographed while perpetrating this small piece of subterfuge. It is at this point of the explanation that the cynically minded could ask shyly why a nonsinging actor would be cast in a musical film in the first place, but such treason must be dismissed quickly.

When faced with the prospect of such a voice double, my theory had always been simple. If a singer could sound like the actor in question when *talking,* then the singing would take care of itself in terms of audience believability. This meant recording the singing experts in a few sentences of spoken script, and proceeding from there. Many extraordinary singers have made handsome sums for being thusly anonymous. The most bizarre instance is famous: The voice double for Lauren Bacall in her debut film, *To Have and Have Not,* was the young Andy Williams. Whether he had to sing higher or lower than was his custom is unknown to me, but it's a verified fact. Since absolutely nothing else of, on, or pertaining to the sensational Miss Bacall has ever had to be faked, the story is pardonable.

During the filming of *Paint Your Wagon* in 1967, it became mercilessly clear that Jean Seberg could not do her own singing. Her speaking voice was soft and modulated, her laugh was like the tinkle of a gamelan orchestra, but her singing was hopeless. The handful of experienced stand-by vocal doubles was quickly auditioned and dismissed as unsuitable in this instance.

One night I was in front of the television, yawning my way through an old musical, when Jeanne Crain, the leading lady of the epic, assayed a love song. It was terrific singing, but patently obviously not her own voice. The more I listened, the more I grew convinced that this voice could be the answer to our current problem. The next morning I rang the music department of Twentieth Century Fox, referred to the televised movie in question, and asked whether they would give me the name of Miss Crain's voice double.

"Wow, that's a long time ago," said a friendly secretary. "I'll have to do a little research and call you back." About an hour later, the phone duly rang. "It was a girl called Anita Conroy," I was told, "but we have no phone number, just an old address. You must remember that it was a long time ago."

I had never heard of Miss Conroy, but it seemed a shame to possibly do her out of a lucrative assignment without exhausting the possibilities of reaching her. Without a phone number, I was forced to send a telegram to the old address. I called Western Union.

"I'd like to send a telegram to a Miss Anita Conroy, please. Her address—"

I was interrupted by the Western Union girl. "Anita Conroy?" she asked. "Would you spell that name for me?"

I was taken aback. "Spell it?" I asked. "Anita Conroy? I'm not pronouncing a Welsh name, miss. It's spelled just as it sounds. Anyway," I went on, "her address is the Sycamore Apartments on—"

Again I was interrupted. "Did you say Sycamore Apartments? Anita Conroy, Sycamore Apartments?"

I grew restive. "Yes, that's what I said, do you perhaps find something peculiar in the name and address?"

"Well, yes I do," said the voice slowly. *"I'm* Anita Conroy and I live at the Sycamore Apartments. Who are you?"

The hair on the back of my neck started tingling, and the walls of my home vibrated with the theme music to *Twilight Zone.* I identified myself with some difficulty and asked whether she had indeed sung for Jeanne Crain in a film.

"Yes, that was me all right," said the voice.

We talked a few minutes. She had experienced an almost total standstill of her career some years ago, times were tough, she was waiting around, she had taken a temporary job answering the phone for Western Union. Was she interested in coming to my office at Paramount the next day to see if her voice would fit Jean Seberg's?

Yes, of course she was.

And she did. And we hired her. And she made quite a bit of money. And what do you think about that!

By now it must be clear that I have led a variety of musical lives and have enjoyed a giant potpourri of professional situations. In the current argot of the recording industry, an artist who makes a "crossover" record is one who might appeal to more than one area of the market. It is an odd and somewhat patronizing addition to the vocabulary, but if the image is valid, then I have crossed not only over, but under as well, and crossed sideways and next to, and have tunneled underground, and bounced on a trampoline. There has always been someone to criticize this facet of my life. Why-don't-you-just-conduct? is thrown at me often. Why-don't-you-just-compose? is another. Why can't you be content playing the piano? Why didn't you concentrate on jazz? Why do you have to try to do so many different things?

I suppose the answer is that I do it out of sheer selfishness. I like doing as many things as possible, as many as I am allowed to try. I adore just about every kind of music making there is. No, wait, I can't stand Hawaiian music—all that flabby guitar-whining puts my teeth on edge. But surely that's a tiny exception to which I am entitled. Everything else, if it's well written or well performed, excites and enlightens me, and makes me want to attempt it myself. This catholicity of taste (or lack of single-mindedness, depending on your point of view) has also enabled me to meet, and sometimes befriend, a great variety of people, all of whom I would have regretted not knowing. Which brings me—circuitously, God knows—to an amazing personality I knew quite well in the 1950s, the comedian Lenny Bruce.

In 1954, I was taking two weeks off from MGM and had gone to San Francisco in order to appear with my jazz trio at a club called New Facks, on Market Street. The other half of the bill was Lenny Bruce. We became instant friends and hung out together from time to time away from the club. Yes, he was most certainly a junkie, and a bad one at that. But never, never did he indulge in anything in front of me; I never saw him pursue his habit. He was, in fact, loyal and thoughtful.

His sense of humor, on the other hand, was completely wild. While he was doing his act in the club, I used to stand in the wings in order to watch every show; he loved playing to musicians, even at the expense of the rest of the audience, and he rarely repeated a piece of business. One night the place was sold out, and Lenny was cruising around the floor, microphone in hand, maniacally zinging everyone in sight. Suddenly he saw a ringside table with two young girls seated by themselves. *"Hi, girls!"* he began. "You here alone? You like the show? What are you doing later?" Giggle giggle from the young ladies. "Well, what about it," Lenny went on. "You wanna go out later or not?"

A hesitant, smothered, giggling nod from one of them.

"Great," enthused Lenny. He looked around and spotted me in the shadows on the side.

"Hey André," he trumpeted, "you wanna get laid later?"

There was no stopping him. We were out on a walk one afternoon, headed toward a coffee house. We passed a lovely book store, Books Inc., on Sutter Street. There, in a window, were the three volumes of Emily Anderson's translations of Mozart's letters. My eyes widened with desire. Then I saw the price tag: ninety dollars. At the time, it might as well have been nine hundred. I bemoaned my lack of funds, put the books out of my head, and Lenny and I proceeded to the coffee house of our choice. As soon as we sat down, Lenny excused himself "for a minute" and took down the street at a clip. I mildly wondered what he was up to, but it was best not to ask questions. After a short while he returned. He opened his overcoat and triumphantly brought out the three volumes of Mozart letters. "Here, man," he said, "I brought you a present. I stole them for you."

I was genuinely shocked. My conservative and fairly narrow-minded upbringing reared its head. "You mustn't do that," I sputtered, an imitation of Dennis the Menace's father. "Stealing!! I can't accept these, I know you meant well but you were wrong, Lenny, really!"

Lenny's reaction was an eye-opener. He was truly and deeply angry. "You're not thinking straight, man," he hissed at me. "If I had ninety bucks and spent it in order to get you a present, what would be the big deal in that? It wouldn't even make a dent in me! But to steal 'em for you—I'm already on parole, man, and if I had got caught, I would have gone back to jail! Now *that's* what I call giving you a present!!"

I felt chastized. I thanked him. Then I took out a pen and asked him to sign the books for me. He grinned from ear to ear, happy again. Here is what he wrote on the fly leaf of the first volume:

$90.00 [he crossed out this figure, and wrote underneath:]
$50.00 [crossed out again]
$12.00 [another heavy line through the price]
$3.00 [crossed again, followed by] 35 cents. [This final handwritten price was amended to read:] "Take it, schmuck, no one's looking. Love from Lenny."

I treasure these books. Not only have I read them and used them for research, but I think I am safe in saying that I own the only set of Mozart's letters signed and stolen by Lenny Bruce.

NINE

IT WAS ALL a very long time ago. Sometimes I have deluded myself into thinking that it all *seems* a long time ago, but viewed in a colder light, it just *was.* Certainly there are elements that have not changed in Hollywood; perhaps a few of the new executives or studio heads feel themselves allied to the old guard, successors to the former rulers; possibly there are a few stars who still exist in a cocoon of self-absorption. But the great difference between now and then must be the fact that everyone currently in the film business is aware of being temporary. This wasn't the case in the days of which I've written, nor was it in the decades before my time. Everything seemed permanent and forever and secure. Joan Crawford didn't envisage studio lots being sold off for real estate, and neither did the prop men. Louis B. Mayer couldn't have imagined the sound stages being empty, and neither could the cops at the gate. And actually, how could they have? Why would any of them have contemplated change? The actors and actresses who were elevated to stardom, or even to long-range contracts, adjusted themselves perfectly to the unreality. Taking a limousine from a sound stage to the commissary for lunch, at most a three-minute walk, seemed not only logical but their just due.

It wasn't their fault; they were trained to think this way. Just about everyone's childhood is a series of unfulfilled desires; wishes that were replaced by new ones as soon as the old ones had been gratified. It's an existence that takes its leave after the first ten years of life, nudged by reality and the need for a more disciplined life.

And here were the big studios, anxious and eager to reinstate these childhood dependencies, insulating their favorites in a dream world, and all this within the confines of an almost flawless atmosphere of materialism. Quite a trick.

There was no reason for any of the big-studio employees to feel the shadow of encroaching *Götterdämmerung*. Life was secure and the studio took care of everything. Automobiles, homes, clothes, photos, trips, secretaries, all were seen to and supplied. Scandals never reached the papers if it could possibly be avoided. All that was asked in return was complete allegiance to the studio, total acceptance and dependence, and since the Faust legend never had been much of a best-seller, there were few arguments. It was this environment into which I was plunged at the age of sixteen. Of course I loved it, and of course I had a good time. It was all very different in the days of my studio work. If nothing else, it was busy, humming with activity and bursting with future plans. Within the confines of purely technical, musical information, I learned the value of disciplined work schedules, of meeting deadlines, of doing technically acceptable work, I learned how to rehearse and how to conduct a large orchestra and how to get along with wildly differing people. I learned how to see the humor in an otherwise deadly situation, and I learned to see the seriousness behind a triviality. I learned to keep my eyes and ears open and how to assimilate the work of my betters. I learned that large houses with snow-white living rooms did not often represent enviable homes, and that the definition of success should not be confined to the work of the past single year. I found out that for every colorful charlatan there existed a reticent talent, that sincerity and integrity are not the same, and that to agree with a popular opinion is not always necessary.

BUT WHY did I leave Hollywood?

Toward the end of my movie career when I had won a few Oscars, Johnny Green, the head of Metro's music department, suggested that I score Joe Pasternak's next musical extravaganza. Joe turned the suggestion down out of hand. Johnny was bewildered. My credits were good and I was reliable and quick; what was wrong? Joe was candid. "I don't want André. He always makes me think my fly is open."

I am not proud of having made Joe feel that way. The truth is I was, in the sixties, somewhat of a misfit in Hollywood, or at least that's how I increasingly came to view myself. It was not an entirely new feeling.

Somewhere back in the early fifties, MGM made a film called *Rhapsody,* which was based unrecognizably on a prolix three-volume novel by Henry Handel Richardson. One memorable moment for the musicians in the audience occurs when Elizabeth Taylor, portraying a brilliant young pianist at conservatory, comes into a coffee shop and sinks down in a booth, obviously spent, overworked, and generally in a frazzle. "Oh, I'm really exhausted," she moans, her head down on the Formica. "That Sibelius piano concerto is killing me," and her fellow students nod sympathetically. The fact that Sibelius never wrote a piano concerto is basic knowledge, and I have wondered ever since why no one caught this kind of blatant inaccuracy. Why didn't someone point it out to the writer? Or to the director? Why didn't one of the poor actors say, "Hey, we can't say that," or why didn't the film editor excise it? How about at the first screening for a theater full of people? Did everybody keep mum out of ignorance or out of fear for his job? There have been countless, collectible lines of dialogue pertaining to music. Joan Crawford to Conrad Veidt, champagne glass in hand: "I like *all* symphonies, *some* concertos, and Chopin before George Sand made him soft." Now I mean!! They don't hardly write dialogue like that no more.

The music tracts for the aforesaid *Rhapsody* were made by a very uptown cast. Claudio Arrau played the piano, and Michael Rabin was the brilliant young violinist whose meteoric career was to be cut so short by his suicide. One day, in the studio commissary, I was seated at a table with both Arrau and Rabin. They were in animated conversation, in which I did not dare join, and of which I was so envious that I couldn't have spoken anyway without choking. The two artists were indulging in traveling virtuoso reminiscences and opinions. There were shouts of laughter about the thirty-three steps an artist must descend in order to reach the stage of the Concertgebouw in Amsterdam, stories of the latest conductor insults hurled at the podium by the principal oboe in the New York Philharmonic, and recollections of the duty-free shops in the

Zurich airport. I was jealous and forlorn and depressed. Would I ever be able to share these stories? Would I ever get beyond the Burbank border patrol in order to give concerts? It all seemed impossibly remote at the time, and I still smart at the memory.

IN FACT, my days in Hollywood had a very undramatic close. I had been doing more and more concerts and I had become absolutely sure that I did not want to spend the rest of my life manufacturing music that would be played while Debbie Reynolds spoke. God knows I had been at it long enough. I had had fun, my assignments had been fairly interesting, I had won four Oscars, and I had a pretty house. But I was ambitious for different pursuits, and I wanted to be involved in work which would frighten me. My film work left me relaxed and complacent, and I wanted to be scared and worried about my music. My final moments in a studio were mild and unheroic. I had accepted an assignment to compose the music for a film at 20th Century-Fox, and I was in the office of its producer, Arthur Jacobs. Arthur had several foibles worth noting: He kept his offices at 30 degrees, in other words at freezing level, and drank a case of iced Coca-Cola a day. He was exclusively geared to movies; seeing live actors on a stage bored him, and reading anything that wasn't mimeographed on pink and blue pages unnerved him. On this particular day, I was explaining a notion I had for the score, and Arthur had not understood the idea. He was dismissive.

"Wait a minute," I heard myself pleading. "Here, read this scene in the script and then I'll explain my idea again."

Arthur picked up the script and began to read. And suddenly it hit me; he was *moving his lips as he read*. His lips actually formed each word as it passed his eyes. A curious thing happened to me; I stood outside myself and watched the scene, Arthur and I in that icy room, while I waited for his reaction, and suddenly, with almost three-dimensional clarity I thought, "I am standing in a room watching a man move his lips while he reads and when he's through reading I'm going to argue music with him." When he looked up, I was ready.

"Arthur," I began, "you won't understand this, I'm not sure I do, but I'm going home now and I don't want to do your picture. And don't worry, I'm not going to work on a different one for someone else, and thanks very much for asking for me, and I'm sorry but I'm leaving town now, because, because . . ." I couldn't think in organized sentences and finished completely lamely, ". . . because, er, I'm going home now."

And so I put my house on the market, and turned my attention to making music elsewhere. I've never been sorry that I worked in Hollywood; I met vastly talented and gifted people—artists—and I learned a great deal. Would I do it again? No. Would I prefer never having done it? No, not at all. It seems now that it was almost a different lifetime, but I wouldn't have missed it.

HAVE I EVER BEEN TEMPTED to go back? Early in 1989 I was on tour in the Far East when I received a cable from the Walt Disney organization telling me that they were planning a brand-new *Fantasia*, not a remake, but a whole new concept, with new pieces of music, and they wanted to discuss my being the new version's Stokowski and conducting all the music. The offer—no, suggestion—made me very happy. I was a big fan of the old 1940 film and felt that it had changed uncountable thousands of young people's minds about classical music. Yes, of course there had been curious lapses in the movie: the cast of sexless cutie pies cavorting in the heavens to the strains of Beethoven's *Pastorale* was sickening, but generally speaking, the film had been quite a triumph. More to the point, the idea of a new version had been proposed to me months earlier by a gifted and funny writer named Bill Dial, who worked for Disney and who was a gigantic music fan and an inveterate concertgoer. In fact, Bill had come to England to see me about the idea, we had made long lists of suggested pieces, and he had come up with extremely apt and clever story ideas for the animation department.

So, when this telegram found me in Hong Kong, I naturally put two and two together, forgetting that I had never been any good at math. Faxes and telexes flew back and forth across the Pacific, with the studio imploring me to drop everything and hurry to California for a meeting. What time would my plane land in Los Angeles? In the morning? Could I come that afternoon? Oh, you suffer from jet lag and want to see your family? Well, it can possibly wait until the following day.

And so, finally I presented myself at the home of Mr. Jeff

Katzenberg, second in command at Walt Disney Productions. I have, in the course of my life and career, been in some pretty large houses, some exquisite and some dreadful, but I had never seen anything quite like this one. It made Versailles look like a tool shed. My footsteps echoed in the foyer and I think I crossed the Bridge of Sighs in order to get to the sitting room. I was greeted with genuine enthusiasm by Mr. Katzenberg, who is young, frighteningly energetic, and in the kind of physical shape that Jane Fonda can only dream of. Quite obviously the young man does five hundred push-ups before each meal, and all without taking the telephone from his ear. During the hour I spent with him, he fielded at least ten business calls, but managed to actually carry on his conversation with me at the same time. It was weird but impressive.

He got right down to brass tacks. "Next year will be the fiftieth anniversary of *Fantasia,* and we'd like to make a brand new one, new music, new stories, up-to-date animation and recording techniques, and you can record it with any orchestra you choose, either in Europe or here."

I was speechless. This really was the new brand of executive I had heard so much about: incisive, determined, artistically in the know, aware of the power of the cinema.

"Sounds great," I managed.

"Now let's talk about repertoire," he went on. "I saw those lists you and Bill Dial made up, but we got us a problem. Yeah, a problem, but I think I've got it solved." He leaned back in his chair and smiled winningly. "See, frankly, I gotta tell you, there's not a single solitary piece of classical music that knocks my socks off." He now leaned toward me, a TV evangelist ready for the commercial. "At first that realization stopped me. But then I thought, well, what does the word 'classic' mean? Doesn't it mean something that will never die?"

I made some sort of noise that could have been interpreted as assent.

"Okay, well, then there's only one kind of music written in the twentieth century that definition can be applied to, the only music since 1900 that will live forever, and do you know what that is?" His look was triumphant, and he waited a beat before delivering the key to the absolute.

"The Beatles!!" and he sank back, a man fulfilling his destiny.

During the ensuing silence I tried to frame various answers ranging from "What are you, crazy?" to "Why haven't I ever thought of that?" with stopovers to commiserate with Stravinsky, Strauss, Ravel, Debussy, Copland, Shostakovich, Prokofiev, Rachmaninoff, and Britten. I think my actual answer was some sort of peevish, "I can't really agree with you on that," but it was not nearly enough to stem the flow of young Katzenberg's adrenaline.

"What we want you to do is to make two hours' worth of symphonic arrangements of the Beatles' songs," he enthused. "No one can do it better than you, and it'll be a fabulous success, there'll be the movie itself and then all those spin-offs—records, videos, T-shirts, games, cereals . . ."

Here was a man with a true vision. This was a crusade. I was completely nonplussed. How could I explain? Of course the idea of Disney animating a film to the Beatles' songs was probably a commercial certainty, but what did it have to do with *Fantasia,* and what did I have to do with it?

The rest of the story is, of course, anticlimactic. I said no; he said lots of money; I said that's not the point although thank you very much; he said can't we change your mind; I said not really but I sincerely wish you every success; he said I sincerely thank you for coming and would you like a drink before you leave?

And so I left, the echo of my footsteps louder than before. I can't quibble with Mr. Katzenberg; his enthusiasm was genuine, his manners impeccable. I guess what depressed me was that it may have been thirty-odd years later, but essentially I had lived through the same scene I had witnessed at MGM when I was the new boy in school.

I wonder what it would feel like to wander the streets of MGM today. I have always avoided class reunions of any sort, shuddering at the very thought. I am told that MGM now consists of one large office building. Gone are the back lots, the village street, the railway station, the French countryside block, the stream with its bridge, the Andy Hardy town, Versailles, and the *Mayflower* swimming in a giant tank. The school houses are gone, as are the rehearsal halls, the recording stages, the Esther Williams pool, and the Western streets. I doubt whether any of these absences would provoke nostalgia in me any more than the moving of Disneyland might. But I would look for, and miss, all the gifted, talented, helpful people who made the decade I spent in Culver City so amazing.

Since leaving Hollywood, I have had the healthy and sobering experience of constantly working with music that is invariably better than any performance of it can be. It keeps final goals always out of reach and it means that boredom is a very rare occurrence. I have always found it necessary for my work to scare me. It doesn't do any good to be totally secure in the knowledge that tomorrow's efforts will not be too difficult, and that they will, with rare exception, be accepted with praise. Nowadays, worry and self-doubt are roommates of mine. I'm frightened by the glory of the music I have to work with, and plagued by personal inadequacies. In my profession, triumphs and failures are allowed to be more private, and mass opinions neither make nor break a lifetime career.

My Academy Award statuettes stand in the corner of a bookcase, and they quite often badly need dusting. Of course it would have been much more valuable if I had been given the unassailably correct tempos for the major works of Mozart as a prize, but nevertheless, I have to say that I can't consider my ten years in Hollywood as any kind of waste. They were entertaining and educational and highly paid, and I am thankful for all that.

Those days are as gone as the old South, and I am awfully glad to have lived through a few of them.

ANDRÉ PREVIN

Films

The Sun Comes Up	1949	
Challenge to Lassie	1949	
Scene of the Crime	1949	
Border Incident	1949	
Tension	1949	
Kim	1950	
The Outriders	1950	
Three Little Words	1950	*
Violent Hour	1950	
Shadow on the Wall	1950	
Cause for Alarm	1951	
Small Town Girl	1953	
The Girl Who Had Everything	1953	
Kiss Me Kate	1953	*
Give a Girl a Break	1953	
Bad Day at Back Rock	1954	§
Kismet	1955	
It's Always Fair Weather	1955	*
The Fastest Gun Alive	1956	
The Catered Affair	1956	
Invitation to the Dance	1956	‡
House of Numbers	1957	
Designing Women	1957	
Silk Stockings	1957	
Hot Summer Night	1957	
Gigi	1958	†
Porgy and Bess	1959	†

Who Was That Lady?	1960	
The Subterraneans	1960	
Bells Are Ringing	1960	*
Elmer Gantry	1960	*
The Four Horsemen of the Apocalypse	1961	
All in a Night's Work	1961	
One, Two, Three	1961	
Two for the Seesaw	1962	*
Long Day's Journey into Night	1962	
Irma La Douce	1963	†
Dead Ringer	1964	
Goodbye Charlie	1964	
My Fair Lady	1964	†
Kiss Me Stupid	1964	
Inside Daisy Clover	1965	
The Fortune Cookie	1966	
Thoroughly Modern Millie	1967	*
Jesus Christ Superstar	1973	*

Apart from the list above, Mr. Previn has worked in various guises on many other films—conducting, writing arrangements or orchestrations, composing without credit given, or writing songs. This list follows:

Holiday in Mexico	1946
Undercurrent	1946
Body and Soul	1947
It Happened in Brooklyn	1947
Fiesta	1947
Song of the Thin Man	1947
The Hucksters	1947
The Other Love	1947
The Pirate	1948
A Date with Judy	1948
The Kissing Bandit	1948
Acts of Violence	1948
The Secret Garden	1949
Malaya	1949
Big Jack	1949

That Forsyte Woman	1949
Above and Beyond	1952
Pepe	1960
Tall Story	1960
Harper	1966
The Swinger	1966
Valley of the Dolls	1967
The Way West	1967
Paint Your Wagon	1969
The Music Lover	1971
Rollerball	1975

*   Academy Award nomination
†   Academy Award
‡   Screen Composers Guild Award
§   Berlin Festival Award

PHOTOGRAPHIC CREDITS

Frontispiece. Alexander Courage.

"With Hedda Hopper . . ." Courtesy of the Academy of Motion Picture Arts and Sciences.

"On the set with Vic Damone and Nat Cole . . ." Courtesy of the Academy of Motion Picture Arts and Sciences, © Turner Entertainment Co., Ren. 1963 Metro-Goldwyn-Mayer Inc. All Rights Reserved.

"My fellow escapee from the sound stages Miklos Rozsa . . ." Alexander Courage.

"A meeting of the Screen Composers Association . . ." André Previn collection.

"Fritz Loewe and Alan Lerner . . ." Photofest.

"My first Oscar . . ." © Copyright Academy of Motion Picture Arts and Sciences.

"My old friend Gene Kelly . . ." © Copyright Academy of Motion Picture Arts and Sciences.

"Billy Wilder, Mike Nichols . . ." André Previn collection.

"With Frank Capp and Red Mitchell . . ." Photofest.

"*The Subterraneans* . . ." Courtesy of the Academy of Motion Picture Arts and Sciences, © 1960 Turner Entertainment Co. & Arthur Freed Productions, Inc., Ren. 1988 Turner Entertainment Co. & Arthur Freed Productions, Inc. All Rights Reserved.

"Remember 'Poetry and Jazz' . . ." Photofest.

"Moonlighting in a jazz club . . ." Courtesy of the Academy of Motion Picture Arts and Sciences, © 1960 Turner Entertainment Co. & Arthur Freed Productions, Inc., Ren. 1988 Turner Entertainment Co. & Arthur Freed Productions, Inc. All Rights Reserved.

"I am obviously exhilarated . . ." Mary Morris Lawrence.

"The Score Board hanging over the orchestra . . ." Mary Morris Lawrence.

"In those days, the London Symphony . . ." Mary Morris Lawrence.

"With Vladimir Ashkenazy at a rehearsal . . ." Mary Morris Lawrence.

"I appear to be controlling traffic . . ." Mary Morris Lawrence.

"Ah, the sixties!" Mary Morris Lawrence.

"My teacher, Pierre Monteux . . ." Mary Morris Lawrence.

"This time the prize was . . ." © Copyright Academy of Motion Picture Arts and Sciences.

"With Debbie Reynolds and the Sherman Brothers . . ." © Copyright Academy of Motion Picture Arts and Sciences.

"This apprehensive-looking Quartet . . ." André Previn collection.

"My old friend Shelly Manne . . ." Robin Lough.

"I was sent this photo by a fan . . ." André Previn collection.

DATE DUE

APR 08 1992			
JUN 09 1992			
JUN 20 1992			
OCT 02 1992			
MY 2 5 '00			
MAR 1 5 2007			
OCT 3 0 2007			
NOV 06 2007			

DEMCO 38-297